Ready for son

* Revelation interpreted like never before.

* A veil of confusion is removed by introducing the *doubled prophecy principle* from Genesis.

* Previously obscure Scriptures gain vital importance.

* Subtle chronology becomes apparent.

* Riddles receive answers from within the Bible.

* Explore what seven thunders uttered.

* Learn how "one" word affects seven seals on a scroll.

* Examine interpretations utilizing Scriptures to explain Scriptures.

* Discover how Jonah clarifies a mystery for "mountains."

* Experience how all "end-time" verses of the Gospels, Epistles and Revelation fuse together to create undeniable chronology, concluding the pre-tribulation vs. post-tribulation rapture debate.

* Analyze why Jesus wears "many" crowns.

* Probe how to apply biblical knowledge received.

* Recognize "Two Women," metaphors for characterizing the people of earth.

TWO WOMEN:

THE BRIDE OF CHRIST,

THE GREAT WHORE:

REVELATION AND MORE

....

BY

THOMAS R. FULTON

3

All Scripture references are from the *Holy Bible*, King James Version (public domain).

All original language references are taken from the *Strong's Exhaustive Concordance of the Bible,* James Strong, Author/Editor.

Printed in the United States of America

Fulton, Thomas R.
Two Women: The Bride of Christ, The Great Whore: Revelation and More

March, 2018

Note of explanation: All direct quotations from Scripture have been written in *italics*. "Emphasis mine" is indicated by words set in **bold print**.

 A doubled prophecy "key" is indicated by the "arrow" symbol.

Please resist the urge to *skim* and *spot read.* Read thoroughly as when reading the Bible; there is an abundance of Scripture included within this book.

* * * * *

I want to express gratitude and appreciation for the wife of my youth supporting and encouraging me. Her time and skills made this book possible.

My special thanks to Claire Fulton for designing the book cover.

Editing contributions are by Linda Stubblefield of *Affordable Christian Editing.*

Table of Contents

SECTION ONE
Introduction

The Bible declares this world is coming to an end. At its conclusion, two groups of people will have been inhabitants; those believing in and depending on God, and those rejecting Him by following natural behavior supported by the devil. In the Gospels, Jesus described those two groups with parables. In one He used the illustration of *sheep* and *goats,* in the other He distinguished *wheat* from *chaff.* In Revelation, they are represented as the *Bride of Christ* and the *Great Whore,* "end-time" characterizations for all of earth's population.

In Revelation, **Jesus** said **seven** times, *"He that hath an ear, let him hear what the Spirit saith unto the churches."*

Do **you** have an ear to hear? Are you ready to be challenged? Are you ready to see how pieces of the Revelation "puzzle" correspond perfectly? Each tab on each puzzle piece fits **precisely** into the next. This writing utilizes the Bible as the main resource to interpret the Bible.

God's Proclaimed Blessing is at the beginning and ending of Revelation.

First Chapter Revelation 1:3	**Last** Chapter Revelation 22:7
*"Blessed is he that **readeth**, and they that **hear** the **words** of this prophecy, and **keep** those things which are **written** therein: for the time is at hand."*	*"Behold, I come quickly: **blessed** is he that **keepeth** the **saying** of the prophecy of this book."*

7

All prophecies of Revelation are important. Understanding the future inspires people to repent and begin close relationship with Christ. God desires His church to have intimate relationship with Him; Revelation becomes a catalyst for relationship. Many people simply want to know when Jesus will return, not caring about the remainder. Those will be short changed and slighted, not knowing its entire content. Do not steal Revelation's effectiveness by telling only bits and pieces; **all prophecies** concerning this book must be explained.

> *"For I testify unto **every man that heareth** the words of the* ***prophecy** of **this book**, If any man shall add unto these things, God shall add unto him the plagues that are written in this book: And if any man **shall take away** from the **words** of the book of **this prophecy**, God shall **take away his part out of the book of life**, and out of the holy city, and from the things which are written in this book"* (Revelation 22:18, 19).

Many viewpoints of others are not presented here, with the same interpretation. A possible explanation is that **previously** it was not God's timing to understand Revelation in this manner. That is why there are concealed mysteries; God **waited** for His scheduled time before allowing comprehension of them.

The method for teaching Revelation is different from other studies (i.e., chapter by chapter). Chapters 1 through 6 are presented in a commentary style. After those chapters, the remainder of Revelation is addressed subject by subject. The reason will become evident to the reader.

Subjects or events are viewed from varying angles (**perspective**). At times an overall "forest-view" is given; at other times, a "close-up" view detailing individual trees is provided. Synonymous words describe subjects addressed more than once. Those are some "keys" employed by this interpretation.

A **master key** unlocks more than one of Revelation's mysteries. This biblical key is discovered in the first book of the Bible. That key is now applied to interpret the last book of the Bible. The principle is plainly stated by the Scripture containing it. Please read Genesis 41:1-32.

The account is about Joseph being brought before Pharaoh to interpret the ruler's two dreams. One dream involved kine (cattle), the other involved corn. Joseph declared the dreams of Pharaoh were prophetic, *"...The dream of Pharaoh is one: **God** hath showed Pharaoh what he is **about to do"** (v. 25). He also explained, *"And for that the **dream** was **doubled** unto Pharaoh **twice;** it is **because** the thing is **established** by **God,** and **God will shortly bring it to pass"** (v. 32).

Purpose to perceive what Genesis 41 is teaching: when God **reveals** and **doubles** a prophetic message, it means that it is **established**, and will happen in the **near** future! That is the reason this book's interpretation needed to wait for the right timing. God waited until He would *"...shortly bring it to pass"* (v. 32).

The "doubled-prophecy principle" explains relationship of multiple passages in Revelation. It is a **primary** key for this reading. It makes this writing unique from what others have perceived.

Note: the **message content** from both of Pharaoh's dreams was the **same** even though **visuals** were **different** (kine and corn). Revelation likewise contains differing visuals.

Interpretation of Revelation

Revelation 1:3, *"Blessed is he that readeth, and they that hear the words of this prophecy, and keep those things which are written therein: for the time is at hand."*

Believers are **blessed** by Revelation through knowing in **advance** the things that will certainly come to pass. This book will explore **how** to prepare for the end-time **after** the interpretation of Revelation. The book of Revelation will reveal **why** Christians **need** to prepare.

WHAT to Do

Zephaniah 2:3	Luke 21:36
"Seek ye the LORD, all ye meek of the earth, which have wrought his judgment; seek righteousness, seek meekness: it may be ye shall be hid in the day of the LORD's anger."	*"Watch ye therefore, and pray always, that ye may be accounted worthy to escape all these things that shall come to pass, and to stand before the Son of man."*

Both of these passages are within the context of end-time prophecies: *"...the day of the LORD's anger"* (Zephaniah 2:3) and Jesus' explanation to His disciples of the end-time (Luke 21).

Remember those two passages of Scripture and be attentive to discover **why** they **exist**. Revelation reveals why.

* * * * *

Chapter 1 of Revelation contains valuable information which is subtle and easily overlooked. Not every reader will appreciate the **technical nature** of the **next few** paragraphs; they are mainly for believers seeking to defend the true faith. These paragraphs will help shield believers from cults that deny the One Triune God. The following analytical approach is **not** employed for the balance of this book.

A basic math principle states that if A = B and B = C then A = C. That principle is exactly how Revelation 1:8, 1:11 and 1:17-18 relate in all *Received Text* (*Byzantine Text*) recensions of the Bible, i.e., the *KJV, NKJV, Young's Literal Translation, Tyndale Bible, J.P. Green's Literal* and so forth. Please note that **modern** translations (post 19th century except *NKJV*) derived from the *Nestle-Aland* (*Alexandrian Text*) translations **leave out** the beginning of verse 11; therefore, an important proof is not contained in **any modern** translations derived from the *Alexandrian Text*. The newer translations also omit words and passages from books other than Revelation. Do **omissions** in modern translations make you wonder **why**?

Following the above proof, Jesus Christ is proven to be **God Almighty**. That confirmation is a dividing point between traditional Christianity and what is considered a cult. In cults, only God is worthy of worship; Jesus is not considered Almighty God and therefore, **He** is not **worthy** of **worship**. Cult followers believe Jehovah God made the statement of being the Almighty in verse 8; however, verse 18 **proves** that it was **Jesus** speaking. Verse 11a (*Received Text* translations) holds the words that **unite** verse 8 with verses 17b and 18, producing evidence and proof. A careful examination of these verses reveals **Who** spoke; consider the following bold print:

Revelation 1:8, *"I am **Alpha and Omega**, the beginning and the ending, saith the Lord, which is, and which was, and which is to*

11

*come, **the Almighty**.*"

Revelation 1:11a: "*I am **Alpha and Omega**, <u>the first and the last</u>...*"

Revelation 1:17b, 18: "*Fear not; I <u>am</u> <u>**the first and the last**</u>: I am **he that liveth, and was dead**; and, behold, I **am alive** for evermore, Amen; and have the keys of hell and death.*"

In Revelation 1:11a, the words *Alpha, Omega, first,* and *last* describe the One speaking them; it also **proves** the **same** Person spoke **all three** verses under consideration. This verse is the direct tie between Revelation 1:8 (*the **Almighty***) and Revelation 1:17b, 18 (*Who liveth, and was **dead*** [Jesus]); it holds a **portion** of **each** verse to **unite** them. *Alpha* and *Omega* is the "Almighty" from verse 8; *first* and *last* is Who "was dead, but is alive"—Jesus, from verses 17b, 18. Those verses **prove** that **Jesus Christ is God Almighty**. Due to their relationship, Jesus **cannot be stripped** of deity.

Those promoting "modern" translations claim the *Received Text* "added" words and verses throughout the New Testament. Those adhering to the *Received Text* claim words and verses were "omitted" from the *Nestle-Aland Text* and its translations. What should conservative believers do when the dispute of verse 1:11a spawns debate about the deity of Jesus? Open **any** translation from either *Nestle-Aland* or *Received Text* to Revelation 22:13, "*I am **Alpha and Omega**, the beginning and the end, the **first and the last**.*" Even **modern** translations read the **same** way. All words describe the same person—Jesus. Whoever removed the passage from Revelation 1:11 many years ago must have **forgotten** about Revelation 22:13; that verse **proves** the phrase should be included in chapter 1—not omitted. Jesus is worthy of **worship** as **Almighty** God!

The above evidence proving error in modern translations should be considered when a believer is deciding which text to follow for other areas of textural inconsistency.

Below is further detail concerning the textural dispute; readers can opt-out of this section if it is not of interest to them.

After the first century, heretical doctrines were infiltrating the church. Gnosticism and other groups formed what traditional Christianity identifies as cults. Heretical groups are the reason early Christian leaders developed "church creeds." The creeds established brief overviews of true Christian faith so that people would not be deceived into believing twisted doctrines.

The Gnostics and other heretics copied **portions** of biblical papyri and then added their own spiritual teachings to the writings. (An internet search of early church heretics will identify the numerous groups.) Heretics dissected Christian writings and then made proselytes in their doctrines. The biblical "canon" was not established and no one could stop them. The writings of the heretical groups are not biblical. They contain biblical passages, but only portions they wanted to include.

The *Alexandrian Text* papyri were discovered in Egypt, the home of Gnosticism. Egypt is the same locality where the *Gospel of Thomas* and other spurious (non-canonical) writings were discovered. Modern translations originate from papyri native to a region known for textural mutilation. That is a probable explanation for the omission of words and verses when comparing modern translations with *Received Text* translations.

Because Egyptian fragments are older, some scholars believe the *Alexandrian Text* (*Nestle-Aland*) is superior. The papyri were discovered in an arid environment, so moisture did not deteriorate them as rapidly as texts native to other ancient regions, thus, they are older.

When Jerome translated the Latin Vulgate (Catholic Bible) around 400 AD, he used the *Byzantine Text*.

Numerically, most of the early church accepted *Byzantine* (*Received Text*) wording; it is **also** referred to as "The Majority Text" because it vastly outnumbers fragments of the *Alexandrian*. Currently, totaling all biblical papyri known to exist, the *Alexandrian Text* comprises less than 20%, the *Byzantine Text* is close to 80%, thereby known as "The Majority Text." Today's church doctrine should be derived from the widely accepted *Byzantine, Received Text*. (An internet search for Byzantine and Alexandrian Text will verify the above percentages.)

* * * * *

Revelation 1:12-17, *"And I turned to see the voice that spake with me. And being turned, I saw seven golden candlesticks; And in the midst of the seven candlesticks one like unto the Son of man, clothed with a garment down to the foot, and girt about the paps with a golden girdle. His head and his hairs were white like wool, as white as snow; and his eyes were as a flame of fire; And his feet like unto fine brass, as if they burned in a furnace; and his voice as the sound of many waters. And he had in his right hand seven stars: and out of his mouth went a sharp two-edged sword: and his countenance was as the sun shineth in his strength. And when I saw him, I fell down at his feet as dead. And he laid his right hand upon me, saying unto me, Fear not; I am the first and the last."*

Those verses no longer portray the Lamb of God slain by crucifixion to atone for sin. They now reveal the Almighty KING OF KINGS AND LORD OF LORDS; He is to be feared and reverenced! John, one of Jesus' dearest disciples, was overwhelmed by His sight and didn't have enough strength to stand.

At His return, **that** is the Jesus **everyone** will see!

THE CHURCHES

THE CHURCH OF EPHESUS

The seven churches of Revelation 2 and 3 represent the people of faith living when the Church Age ends. Some believe the seven churches are meant to apply in different historical time periods. The conclusion of this chapter will bring comprehension.

Revelation 2:1-7, *"Unto the angel of the church of Ephesus write; These things say he that holdeth the seven stars in his right hand, who walketh in the midst of the seven golden candlesticks; I know thy works, and thy labour, and thy patience, and how thou canst not bear them which are evil: and thou hast tried them which say they are apostles, and are not, and hast found them liars: And hast borne, and hast patience, and for my name's sake hast laboured, and hast not fainted. Nevertheless I have somewhat against thee, because thou hast left thy first love. Remember therefore from whence thou art fallen, and repent, and do the first works; or else I will come unto thee quickly, and will remove thy candlestick out of his place, except thou repent. But this thou hast, that thou hatest the deeds of the Nicolaitanes, which I also hate. He that hath an ear, let him hear what the Spirit saith unto the churches; To him that overcometh will I give to eat of the tree of life, which is in the midst of the paradise of God."*

The Church of Ephesus performed good works for service to God. In verse 2 Jesus said, *"I know thy works* [toil as effort or occupation] *and thy labour* [toil—to reduce strength] *and thy patience...."* *Patience* is again mentioned in verse 3 as reference to how people held on, not losing motivation; they endured even through tough hardships. No one needs patience when everything is going great. The people in Ephesus were enduring trials.

Verses 4 and 5 indicate that **regardless** of good works and service, something displeased God. He is dissatisfied enough to remove their candlestick. In Revelation 1:13, 20, Jesus walks in the midst of seven candlesticks which are the seven churches. Jesus is there in the churches, similar to God manifesting in the temple. Simply put, the church of Ephesus could become as the temple of Jerusalem, desolate of God (Luke 13:35). From that point, there would be no life of God; His presence would be removed. Jesus is **warning** the Ephesians to prevent that from happening to them.

What went wrong? The answer is found in verse 4; Jesus said, *"...thou hast left thy first love."* They neglected the first and greatest commandment; it is supposed to be the **focus** of **Christian faith**!

> Mark 12:29, 30, *"And **Jesus** answered him, The **first of all the commandments is**, Hear, O Israel; The Lord our God is one Lord: And thou shalt love the Lord thy God with all thy heart, and with all thy soul, and with all thy mind, and with all thy strength: this is the **first commandment**."*

Those verses have great **authority**; they declare what **God** regards as the **highest** and **greatest** of all commands and laws. Those verses show by **their content**, they **supersede** other Scripture and are to be elevated in importance. Jesus said, *"...this is the first commandment."*

Evaluating the works of Ephesus divulges whether or not the same error may apply to current believers. Christian witness and works are to **flow out of** relationship with God. The witness and works **do not form** a believer's relationship. **Their personal**

relationship with God needs to be first priority! Focusing **primarily** on the "Great Commission" or any "ministry" rather than developing personal, ongoing relationship with God is error. Ephesus' emphasis on winning the lost caused personal, spiritual relationship and character to become secondary in importance to godly works. God wants time, growth and relationship with **Him first**, and **then** the **work** believers do for His church **second**.

The first **priority** for believers is to grow in godliness and learn to "know" God; that is how the "love" of God begins. *"But seek ye first the kingdom of God, and His righteousness…"* (Matthew 6:33), means exactly what it says. God's kingdom (literally: rule/reign) and living righteously must be of **first** importance. That is accomplished through a **precedence** of private prayer, worship and contemplative Bible reading. Time spent in those is to have **supremacy** over works of service **for** God. After correcting the church at Ephesus, Jesus told them to do the *"first works"* (v. 5). He basically said, things people do **for** Him **are important**, but are secondary to developing a personal, maturing relationship **with** Him. The **priority order** of **relationship** vs. **works** was very serious; He would remove their candlestick (His presence) if they did not repent.

Jesus states He hates the **deeds** of the Nicolaitanes. The word *deeds* is the same word translated "**works**" in verse 2: the toil and effort in living day by day. The Nicolaitanes were known for a lifestyle of "spiritual liberty." To express that concept in a different manner, they deemed that since their sins were covered by the blood of Christ, it did not matter how morally they lived. That attitude has been coined as "runaway grace." This attitude is observed in the person who professes he is eternally saved and knows Jesus, but then continues to commit adultery, steal, get drunk, and so forth. **Jesus** said He **hates** that attitude! People exhibiting such an attitude do not love Him with all of their heart, mind, soul and strength.

17

They are **not** putting Jesus **first** in their lives! The Nicolaitanes' type of attitude was addressed in 2 Peter 2:12-22 and Jude 1:8-16.

THE CHURCH OF SMYRNA

The church of Smyrna reveals a difference in value systems regarding God's standard vs. men's.

> Revelation 2:9, *"I know thy works and tribulation, and poverty, (but thou art rich) and I know the blasphemy of them which say they are Jews, and are not, but are the synagogue of Satan."*

The people are in poverty by human standards, yet Jesus says they are rich. Their lives of toil and right deeds were acceptable to Christ. Their eternal rewards will be wonderful.

Christians are identified by the name of "Jesus Christ"—the name that is used to call upon God. The same holds true for other faiths that are not Christian. Those who follow Buddha are Buddhists; a Muslim (Islam) looks to Allah. These religions are identified through the name of the god on whom they focus. To honor God, it is best not to speak the names of those false gods (Exodus 23:13, Joshua 23:7).

One congregation of people gathers in the name of Israel's God "Jehovah," but they are **not** under Jewish law or a part of Judaism. They only gather under that name. In effect, they are saying they are Jews, but they are not. Be cautious and stay away from any such group. Jesus' name must be above every name and part of a three-person Godhead. Christians must avoid congregations that are otherwise! Jesus says they are of the devil (v. 9).

18

Revelation 2:10, *"Fear none of those things which thou shalt suffer: behold, the devil shall cast some of you into prison, that ye may be **tried**; and ye shall have **tribulation** ten days; be thou faithful unto death, and I will give thee a crown of life."*

Smyrna is a place of great persecution; some church members have been imprisoned. *"That ye may be **tried**"* means "to be **tested**." *Tribulation* means "to be put under **pressure**." Those believers are "**tested** under **pressure**." The pressure is to be imprisoned and await the death sentence. Jesus told them to be faithful unto death; they would receive a crown of life.

Sometimes tribulation is referenced as the time of distress coming upon unbelievers and those converted to Christianity during the end-time. Though it is understood in that way, that viewpoint is not complete. It is not only a "boxed" period of time; consider the word's definition "to be put under pressure." Pressure often comes upon a person following after God. Contemplate when a little lie can keep someone out of a lot of trouble. Then he remembers God said, *"Thou shalt not lie."* He is faced with tribulation, i.e., "being tried under pressure." What will he do? Will he make it easier on his flesh by lying or obey God and take the consequences for being truthful? Those **consequences** are the **cause** of the **pressure** *(tribulation)* he would like to avoid. God issued this believer a small "test." A huge "test" is on the way.

According to Revelation, God allows **great** tribulation to come upon portions of His church. Those people face the ultimate pressure of having to choose between giving up their physical lives as martyrs, or giving up their eternal souls to hell.

Tribulation is the decision point people are forced to face, whether it is small (moderate consequences) or great (enormous

19

consequences).

Tribulation is **not** God's wrath! In **addition** to tribulation, wrath is dispensed upon unbelievers during the time period covered by Revelation. God's people will **not** be the recipients of His **wrath**, though a group of believers will experience **tribulation**. Those are addressed later.

No correction is recorded for the church of Smyrna. Their doctrine must have been acceptable; nevertheless, they needed to have their **faith** put to the "test" of "pressure."

The responses of a Christian while under the pressures of life reveal his sincerity to faith. All will experience tribulation in one form or another. Sooner or later, everyone will be tempted under pressure to disobey God. What will **you** do when pressure comes upon you?

"Great" tribulation is coming soon. Many people will be put under "great pressure."

THE CHURCH OF PERGAMOS

> Revelation 2:13, *"I know thy works, and where thou dwellest, even where Satan's seat is: and thou holdest fast my name, and hast not denied my faith, even in those days wherein Antipas was my faithful martyr, who was slain among you, where Satan dwelleth."*

Some modern theologians may indicate those words of Jesus were written for John's time; nothing relative to Antipas is known in the current era. The phrase *"even in those days"* reveals God was spanning time and addressing the current church. Today, just as in days of old, societies are permeated by Satan. The passage is relevant at present.

20

Revelation 2:14, *"But I have a few things against thee, because **thou hast** there them that hold the **doctrine of Balaam**, who **taught** Balak to **cast a stumbling block** before the children of Israel, to eat things sacrificed unto idols, and to commit fornication."*

God has a few issues against Pergamos, even though they reverence the Lord's name in a society overrun with wickedness. Jesus refers to the *"doctrine of Balaam"* being among them. What is that? The "doctrine of Balaam" is uncovered through perceiving the following passages:

- In Numbers 24:10-13, Balak wanted to pay Balaam to **curse** Israel. However, when Balaam consulted God, He commanded a **blessing** upon Israel, thereby angering Balak.
- Numbers 24:25 reveals that Balaam and Balak did spend time together and were parting company (after Balak's earlier disappointment).
- In Numbers 25:1-3, Israel sinned greatly and **angered** God; He had previously commanded Balaam to bless Israel. What happened? By intermarrying with pagan people of the surrounding society, God's people were behaving as the Gentiles. Six chapters later, Moses discloses that the intermarriage was actually the counsel of Balaam. Numbers 31:16 says,

*"Behold, **these** caused the children of Israel, **through** the **counsel of Balaam** to commit trespass against the LORD in the matter of Peor, and there was a plague among the congregation of the LORD."*

That is the stumbling block Jesus referred to. Balaam wasn't allowed to curse Israel, but he advised Balak to allow Israel to

21

intermarry with Moabite women. By intermarrying and intermixing pagan morals and society with those of the people of God, Israel became corrupted. Israel had to be separate and live exclusively by God's laws in order to receive His blessings. By **compromising** their **total** dedication, Israel became polluted. God withdrew His blessing; a plague resulted. Jesus is **warning** His **church** of the **same plot** against it—**compromise**, the doctrine of Balaam!

Numerous present-day churches have overshadowed God's Word with human reasoning and cultural values. Many no longer obey God concerning appropriate lifestyle and behavior. Society and advanced education teach people to use intellect. Countless times human reason and God's counsel oppose one another. Various Christians seek the counsel of friends and others; they feel the ways of God are radical and will not obey them. Most people don't realize God's statutes are far above what comes naturally to human behavior (Isaiah 55:7-9).

Many church members behave like unbelievers. They divorce, cheat (especially on taxes), lie (if justifiable by reason), do not speak against abortion (murder), and return wickedness for wickedness in word or deed. Some churches endorse "a safe, alternative Halloween" instead of **refusing** to participate in Satan's holiday. Churches hold "divorce recovery classes" instead of strongly teaching Malachi 2:15, 16: **no divorce; God hates it** (except when caused by adultery [Matthew 19:9]). Some churches even accept "alternate lifestyles" (homosexuality) by **stretching** Jesus' teaching about love to the point of **superseding the importance of scriptural instruction on sin.** Believers are **not to receive** the wicked into the church (1 Corinthians 5:13). Of course, mine is not an exhaustive list, but the point is established.

The **doctrine of Balaam** is functioning in today's church. Presently, leadership is accepting and teaching believers to do what is politically correct by society's standards, rather than adhering strictly to God's standards. Many have thereby COMPROMISED the Word of God.

Numerous Christians living in this current society allow faith to have **some** impact on how they live. Christians **should** live with such radical faith in God that **they** impact society. What is God's remedy for a church compromising standards clearly declared in His Word? The answer: "***Repent****; or else I will come unto thee quickly, and will fight against them with the sword of my mouth*" (Revelation 2:16).

Repenting from compromise will offend people. Believers may be called intolerant, radical or crazy for behaving as Scripture instructs them. No longer can they accept the cultural view of right or wrong to be "politically correct." They must strictly adhere to Scripture and convictions of the Holy Spirit. When reason and logic indicate a type of behavior is acceptable but Scripture requires different behavior, Christians must obey the Word of God, walking by faith rather than sight!

The church of Pergamos not only had mixed values of unbelievers causing it to compromise, but also the Nicolaitanes—believers who alleged it was **acceptable to continue** in ungodly behavior.

The compromising church of the end-time is substantiated in 1 Timothy 4:1, 2:

> "*Now the Spirit speaketh expressly, that **in the latter times** some shall **depart** from the faith, giving heed to seducing spirits, and **doctrines of devils**; Speaking lies and hypocrisy; having their conscience seared with a hot iron.*"

Paul spoke of this era in 2 Timothy 4:3, 4:

> "*For the time will come when **they will not endure sound***

23

*doctrine; but after their own lusts shall they **heap** to*
*themselves **teachers**, having itching ears; And they shall*
***turn away their ears from the truth**, and shall be turned*
unto fables."

Jesus hates the fruits produced by compromise (Revelation 2:15).
Carefully and courageously guard your attitude and faith against
compromise. Ask the Holy Spirit to give you grace to endure.

THE CHURCH OF THYATIRA

Revelation 2:19-25, *"I know thy works, and charity, and*
service, and faith, and thy patience and thy works; and the
last to be more than the first. Notwithstanding I have a few
things against thee, because thou sufferest [permit] that
woman Jezebel, which calleth herself a prophetess, to teach
and to seduce my servants to commit fornication, and to eat
things sacrificed unto idols. And I gave her space to repent
of her fornication; and she repented not. Behold, I will cast
her into a bed, and them that commit adultery with her into
***great** tribulation, except they repent of their deeds. And I*
will kill her children with death; and all the churches shall
know that I am he which searcheth the reins and hearts: and
I will give unto every one of you according to your works.
But unto you I say, unto the rest in Thyatira, as many as
have not this doctrine, and which have not known the depths
of Satan, as they speak; I will put upon you none other
burden. But that which ye have already, hold fast till I
come."

The Lord commended the church of Thyatira. He said they

24

had charity, which is *agapé* **love**; that is a compliment. It is one of the marks of mature teaching. Many modern-day churches focus primarily on the attribute of love. An emphasis on love along with only "positive" messages works very well for numerical growth. The problem is they voluntarily abandon other precepts from God's Word. Messages based on repentance, sexual purity, disciplined lifestyle, honesty, and numerous other statutes are not expounded. Their main focus is acceptable, but no facet of Truth can be neglected. **Incomplete doctrine produces subtle error**, which is the probable flaw in Thyatira.

The church of Thyatira allowed Jezebel to *seduce* them. *Seduce* implies a subtle approach into error rather than bold new theology. Subtle error is more difficult to detect. **Neglect** of Scriptures promoting discipline and obedience produces seduction—subtle error. Paul used the same word *seducing* to describe spirits that infiltrate the end-time church (1 Timothy 4:1); it is a common theme.

Jesus' words in verse 20: *"to commit fornication and to eat things sacrificed unto idols"* proclaims there is sin in Jezebel's doctrine. In the Old Testament, God said Aholah and Aholibah played *"the harlot"* and committed whoredom against Him. They metaphorically represented Israel's split kingdom consisting of Samaria and Judea (Ezekiel 23:1-7). God used metaphorical wording to describe Israel; He is doing the same in Revelation by utilizing the name *Jezebel* to describe His church.

To develop a better insight dictates looking at Jezebel from the Old Testament. 1 Kings chapters 16-21 recount King Ahab and his Zidonian (heathen) wife Jezebel, who worshipped Baal. Ahab was king of Israel, the leader of God's people. He grew to be a wicked king by God's standard; in fact, he was worse than all of his predecessors. Jezebel's influence over him and Israel was manipulative and treacherously against God. She had the true

25

prophets of God killed and used authority gained through her husband to work wickedness. Of all the women named throughout Scripture, no one did more against God than Jezebel. That name is synonymous with manipulation and dominating control over true authority.

Using her name in a church indicates wickedness is present through manipulation. Tainted control is subduing formerly recognized authority and doctrine. The error is introduced through female influence. She calls herself a prophetess (v. 20) and presents doctrine (v. 24). The theology she teaches causes believers to sin. Those who receive her deceptions behave accordingly. The truth of God is corrupted subtly from **inside** the church.

Jesus holds the ones listening to her doctrine **responsible** for their behavior. They *"suffered"* (permitted) her to teach them (v. 20). Those are instructed to *"repent of their deeds"* (v. 22). Behavior is wrong due to corrupted **values**; repentance is needed. They **perform** Christian *love, works,* and *service* with *patience,* but continue in **behavioral** error. That is why Jesus said they were *seduced.*

Whoever continues committing sin is thrown into great tribulation. Again, *tribulation* means "pressure." They are given the choice to live righteously or be placed into *great* pressure. The passage **applies** to the present-day church; "great pressure" is coming in this era.

Jesus spoke concerning churches influenced by Jezebel's doctrine, referring to them as *"her children."* In verse 23, Jesus said those "children" will be killed with death. Jesus is speaking of **churches** that are "children" of false teaching. No literal "people" will die; rather, the denominations or groups which follow the doctrine Jezebel introduced will have a spiritual death.

Can a dead person recognize another dead person? No; life must be present to recognize death. Two bodies in a morgue cannot recognize one another. Jesus said **churches** will recognize "death"—not unbelievers. That is not physical death, but a spiritual one. Only Christians with the Holy Spirit living in them will recognize lack of life in churches which lose God's presence. In spiritually dead churches, ritual void of God's presence will continue. Christians listening to God's Spirit recognize an absence of God's presence and the spiritual death in that church.

Throughout church history from the Apostolic Fathers to the Reformation, I have not found evidence of females leading spiritual gatherings or affecting doctrines of the established church. After the Reformation, there are recorded accounts of separate **ministries** with female leadership, but not in the sense of the "traditional" church. One example is the Salvation Army (mid-1800s); it is not a church, but a mission to the poverty-stricken. William and Catherine Booth were the founders and women are regarded equal to men in authority.

Only since the 1900s have women entered positions that affect doctrine within traditional churches. That fact should help those having doubts to realize, the letters to the seven churches are meant for **this** generation. Ingress of female leadership into the established church **could not** apply for a **different** time period of church history.

God's Word makes the role of women in church very clear.

1 Corinthians 14:34, 35, *"Let your women keep silence in the churches: for it is not permitted unto them to speak; but they are commanded to be under obedience as also saith the law. And if they will learn anything, let them ask their husbands at home: for it is a shame for women to speak in the church."*

Paul did not have an "attitude" because of cultural problems

27

with the women of Corinth as is sometimes taught. He restates that to Timothy as general instruction, never mentioning the Corinthian church.

> *"Let the woman learn in silence with all subjection. But I suffer not a woman to teach, nor to usurp [dominate] authority over the man, but to be in silence"* (1 Timothy 2:11, 12).

By context, those passages refer to the teaching and learning process—doctrine.

Female spiritual leadership is only to be a **rare** exception for an individual ministry (not church), and only **if** God establishes it. It is **not** what God has declared by His Word and is **not** to be "commonplace" as is often observed today. It seems as though, **if God makes a special allowance by His choice**, humans will unwisely say, "Look at so-and-so's ministry and anointing. It is evident that God is doing this even though it is contrary to His Word; we will do it in the church since God started it." That rationale is how some will apply human reasoning to nullify the Word of God.

The problem is that **only God** has the **authority** to call and ordain anyone to a ministry that supersedes what is **written** in His Word. No matter what their titles may be, **people** and reasoning are **never** superior to God's written Word! An ordination for ministry needs to follow His guidelines via all of His Word. If the Bible is the written Word of God, how can men use intellect to make **His Word sterile**? If doing so becomes acceptable with this topic, where will men stop? There will be nothing that Christians can regard as the solid, sacred Word of God upon which to build their lives; all of God's Word will be subject to the rationalizing of men. His Word is not subject to men; rather, men must be subject to His

28

Word. **He** is the One holding **authority**. The church belongs to and is led by Him; it is **not** the property of men with titles. Numerous people of present time need to learn that.

If women are not allowed to be in authority and teach in church, how are they to serve God? Women are instructed to teach the younger women and children, as in accordance with Titus 2:3-5.

Being under male authority pertains to the church and to the home, as stated in Ephesians 5:22, 23, which say,

"Wives, submit yourselves unto your own husbands, as unto the Lord. For the husband is the head of the wife, even as Christ is the head of the church...."

I did not say that; **God** said it through Paul. Also consider the following passages: 1 Corinthians 11:3, 8, 9; 1 Peter 3:1-6, and Colossians 3:12-19.

Women may pray and prophesy in church (1 Corinthians 11:5). They may serve others with their spiritual gifting. They may worship aloud; the "silence" in Scripture pertains to teaching and learning within church gatherings.

Some churches have ignored verses affecting the proper place of women in the church; they claim Galatians 3:28 **nullified** them. *"There is neither Jew nor Greek, there is neither bond nor free, there is neither male nor female: for ye are all one in Christ Jesus."* The context surrounding that verse teaches that every person becomes God's child when he comes to Christ by faith; anyone can come. Nationality, a person's position in society, or gender does not matter and they are no longer under the "law." By **context**, verse 28 **pertains** to **salvation**; **anyone** can be saved and come into the body of Christ. (To verify, read Galatians 3:22, 26-29.)

That Scripture does **not** describe the role or gifting of the

Jew or the Greek, the husband or the wife, or anyone else in the body of Christ. (Colossians 3:10, 11 are similar.) So why does verse 28 say *"...there is neither male nor female: for ye are all one in Christ Jesus"*? That portion of the verse is what some people use to support females having an acceptable place in the leadership realm.

Other Scriptures clarify the meaning of Galatians 3. Paul explains the function of the body as one in unity; then he adds more detail as to how one body operates.

> Romans 12:4, 5, *"For as we have many members in **one body**, and all members have **not** the **same office**: So **we**, being many, **are one** body in Christ, and every one **members one of another.**"*

Paul describes some roles that members of the body of Christ perform in the following verses:

> *"Having then gifts differing according to the grace that is given to us, whether prophesy, let us prophesy according to the proportion of faith; Or ministry, let us wait on our ministering: Or he that teacheth, on teaching; Or he that exhorteth, on exhortation: he that giveth, let him do it with simplicity; he that ruleth, with diligence; he that showeth mercy, with cheerfulness. Let love be without dissimulation. Abhor that which is evil; cleave to that which is good"* (vv. 6-9).

Additional explanation describing the church as consisting of many **individual members** but being **one body** is found in 1 Corinthians 12:12-20. **Roles** are different, but all are **equally** important. Jesus prayed for unity of the **one** body before He was crucified (John 17:20, 21); He wanted the church to be similar to God-Head unity.

30

Those verses show **why** Galatians 3:28 declares it does not matter **who** you are. Believers are **all** "one" in Christ, a place where there is neither male nor female—the **unity** of **one** body.

Galatians 3:28 was **never** meant to **override** and **nullify** other Scripture. If verses of Scripture are continually removed from context to establish doctrine, there will be **no end** to the **abuse** of Scripture. In this instance, people dispute there is no status for male or female; believers are all "one" in God's sight. Those embracing the homosexual lifestyle could use Galatians 3:28 to **argue** that God does **not disapprove** of them; He does not acknowledge the role of male or female. Will that argument, based on **one** Scripture **removed** from its **context**, nullify Scriptures identifying homosexuality as sin? To what measure will people **misuse** God's Word to achieve their desires?

Those adhering to out-of-context interpretations for Scripture infer that God's Word is not sufficient; it needs the help of human intellect. That happened before; the improper use of Scripture and teaching the traditions of men is the reason Jesus corrected the Pharisees.

God's Word does **not contradict** itself. If there appears to be a controversy, the **contexts** of involved verses must be compared. God's Word does **not** give anyone the **option** to choose which verse **he wants** to believe and apply. **All** are valid and must be correctly understood.

The Jezebel spirit pertains to a desire for authority to influence others; it can be desire for formal authority or simply an attempt to dominate while under authority. This Jezebel spirit operates in the church or in the home. That spirit continues to function today. If a woman is not content to serve others but wants to be of great influence through control or leadership, she needs to ask God if she is being affected by the Jezebel spirit.

John was inspired to write Revelation two thousand years

31

ago; God knew the church would fall away from many of His instructions. He knew His Word would be disobeyed and compromised in the area of church leadership along with other areas of doctrine. If His Word was adhered to, a "Jezebel" could never have affected the church.

* * * * *

Some believers in Thyatira were not deceived by Jezebel; they *"...have not known the depths of Satan"* (Revelation 2:24). They only need to continue in the love, service, faith, patience and works the Lord has approved (v. 19); Jesus accepts those without correction. Some behaved righteously; Jesus was pleased.

THE CHURCH OF SARDIS

Revelation 3:1-5, *"And unto the angel of the church in Sardis write; These things saith he that hath the seven Spirits of God, and the seven stars; I know thy works, that thou hast a **name** that thou **livest**, and art **dead**. Be watchful, and strengthen the things which remain, that are **ready** to **die**: for I have not found thy works perfect before God. Remember therefore how thou hast received and heard, and hold fast, and **repent**. If therefore thou shalt not watch, I will come on thee as a thief, and thou shalt not know what hour I will come upon thee. Thou hast a few names even in Sardis which have not defiled their garments; and they shall walk with me in white: for they are worthy. He that overcometh, the same shall be clothed in white raiment; and I will not blot out his name out of the book of life, but I will confess his name before my Father, and before his angels."*

The Lord evaluated Sardis according to how the people lived—that is, by their works. The Greek word *works* is the one denoting the toil and effort of everyday behavior. This time Jesus does not simply have a correction to make to the church. He speaks straightforwardly with them and tells them they are dead (a corpse). They possess the name to have life (Christian), but they are **digressing** in the fruitfulness of godly behavior. In fact, Jesus says their godliness is about to disappear. Christians' lives were supposed to become full and complete in the way of righteousness; their lives were to be fruitful by allowing Jesus to be their author and finisher of faith (Hebrews 12:1, 2). Jesus instructs them to **repent**.

Some believers in Sardis are living uprightly before God. He says they will walk with Him in white; they are not defiled. According to Revelation 19:8, to *"walk in white"* is to be clothed with the righteousness of saints.

Revelation 3:5, *"...I will not blot out his name out of the book of life..."* is a verse some Christians ignore. The doctrine of eternal security has a large following, which is exemplified by "once-saved, always-saved" extreme Calvinist theology. Verse 5 is in **direct opposition** to the doctrine of eternal security and unites with other Scriptures contesting it.

*"While they promised them liberty, they themselves are the servants of corruption: for of whom a man is overcome, of the same is he brought in bondage. For **if** after they have **escaped** the pollutions of the world **through the knowledge of the Lord** and Savior Jesus Christ, they are **again entangled** therein, and **overcome**, the **latter end** is worse with them than the beginning. For **it had been better** for them **not to have known the way of righteousness**, than, after **they have known it, to turn** from the holy*

*commandment delivered unto them. But it is happened unto them according to the true proverb, The dog **is turned** to his own **vomit again;** and the sow that **was washed** to her wallowing in the mire"* (2 Peter 2:19-22).

Hebrews 6:4-6, 10:26-29, and Matthew 13:18-23 also clearly oppose the eternal-security concept that once "saved," no one can fall away from saving faith in Christ.

Is one willing to use a razor knife and remove Revelation 3:5 or other verses from his Bible? To ignore its existence or explain it away as "invalid" is to **remove it doctrinally**. If such behavior is initiated, **where and how is it stopped…once it has begun**? All Scripture must **fit together** like a jigsaw puzzle to show a completed picture. Omitting or invalidating what is clearly written removes vital pieces from the **complete doctrine** of Christian faith. One Scripture cannot supersede another; they **must** blend together.

Some people object to doctrine produced from Revelation because of its metaphors and imagery. That argument cannot be applied in this case. The Lord is able to blot a name out of the Book of Life. Moses knew it was possible although he did not perceive the gravity and significance the Book of Life held. People promoting eternal security do not believe God will blot out a name; they contest what **God Himself has established**! On judgment day, they will have to explain why they are right and God is wrong. Look at Exodus 32:31-33:

*"And Moses returned unto the LORD, and said, Oh, this people have sinned a great sin, and have made them gods of gold. Yet now, if thou wilt forgive their sin—; and if not, blot me, I pray thee, out of thy book which **thou hast written**. And the **LORD said** unto Moses, Whosoever hath sinned against **me**, **him will** I **blot out of** my **book.**"*

Revelation did **not** establish that doctrine; God's **quoted** Word did. Revelation clearly carried the doctrine from the Old and into the New Testament; it is valid for the church.

There are those believing the warning letters to churches do not apply to the present-day church. They would say, "Those letters are not necessary for us; we possess salvation." In their viewpoint, since salvation is a gift from God, it is a commodity—something tangible that has been given and therefore will never be taken away. They use emotional sermons, a **select** group of Scriptures and human logic to assert their viewpoint.

They may allege that Christians cannot lose "salvation" because they are predestined by the will of God (Romans 8:29, 30; Ephesians 1:5). True, God calls many to salvation; He makes sure they are born or live in a place where the gospel message reaches them (predestined). Once they **receive** the message, they must grow into the **image** of Jesus (Romans 8:29). If they are **not willing** to be conformed into His image, what happens? The disciples of Jesus are an example, *"And **we believe** and are **sure** that **thou art** that **Christ**, the Son of the living God. Jesus answered them, Have not I **chosen** you twelve, and one of you is a devil"* (John 6:69, 70)? Let God's Spirit and Word direct doctrine—not human arguments or emotions.

Do not view salvation as a commodity. Believe **all** related Scriptures, combining them in order to reveal more complete knowledge. According to Jesus' words, salvation is a straight and narrow path (Matthew 7:14). A Christian begins walking that path when the Lord calls (predestines) him to salvation and the offer to "be saved" is accepted. The path **leads** to eternal life. *"Because strait is the gate, and narrow is the way, which **leadeth** unto life, and few there be that find it."* The course must be completed; God's correction and direction (grace) are needed to keep a believer on the right path.

Christians have a part to play within salvation, repentance from sin. *"Having therefore these promises, dearly beloved, let us* **cleanse ourselves** *from* **all filthiness** *of the flesh and spirit,* **perfecting holiness** *in the* **fear** *of God"* (2 Corinthians 7:1). That verse portrays an attitude in agreement with Philippians 2:12, which says; *"...work out your own* **salvation** *with* **fear** *and trembling."*

Some people may respond from Scripture that *"...* **perfect** *love casteth out* **fear**,*"* referring to 1 John 4:18. That is Scripture, so it is true, but examine the verse closely. Living Christian lives in perfected love will remove fear, but only **perfect** ("mature, sincere, complete, of full age") love removes fear. Many believers do not live through all the circumstances of life and habitually behave according to the traits **Scripture** describes as "love."

> *"Charity* [love] *suffereth long, and is kind; charity envieth not; charity vaunteth not itself, is not puffed up. Doth not behave itself unseemly, seeketh not her own, is not easily provoked, thinketh no evil; Rejoiceth not in iniquity, but rejoiceth in the truth; Beareth all things, believeth all things, hopeth all things, endureth all things. Charity never faileth..."* (1 Corinthians 13:4-8).

Until this passage describes each individual's character, they still **need** a **reverential, holy fear** of **God!**

> *"Wherefore we receiving a kingdom which cannot be moved, let us have grace, whereby we may serve God acceptably with* **reverence and godly fear***: For our God is a consuming fire"* (Hebrews 12:28, 29).

Failing to fully understand God's love will not send someone to hell; failing to understand and fear His wrath... might.

Both must be taught.

"And of some have compassion, making a difference: And others save with fear, pulling them out of the fire; hating even the garment spotted by the flesh" (Jude 1:22, 23).

There are people calling themselves Christians but fail to have reverential, godly fear. *"These are spots in your feasts of charity, when they feast with you, feeding themselves **without fear**..."* (Jude 1:12).

THE CHURCH OF PHILADELPHIA

Revelation 3:7-11, *"And to the angel of the church in Philadelphia write; These things saith he that is holy, he that is true, he that hath the key of David, he that openeth, and no man shutteth; and shutteth, and no man openeth; I know thy works: behold, I have set before thee an open door, and no man can shut it: for thou hast a little strength, and hast kept my word, and hast not denied my name. Behold, I will make them of the synagogue of Satan, which say they are Jews, and are not, but do lie; behold, I will make them to come and worship before thy feet, and to know that I have loved thee. Because thou hast kept the word of my patience, I will also keep thee from the hour of **temptation**, which shall come upon all the world, to **try** them that dwell upon the earth. Behold, I come quickly: hold that fast which thou hast, that no man take thy crown."*

The church of Philadelphia has been commended. Jesus approves of their works (lifestyle) and lets them know He is directing them, opening doors no one can close.

The Philadelphia church has not denied Jesus' name; He is worthy of worship, being part of the Triune Godhead. Jesus says those who identify themselves as Jews (Jehovah's name) but are not Jews, will be shown to be in error—like the ones of Smyrna (Revelation 2:9). Those false Jews following Satan in wickedness against Christ will bow before the Philadelphia church (v. 9).

Jesus keeps Philadelphia from the *"hour of temptation."* **Temptation** is defined as "putting to proof by experiment of good or evil." The temptation is to **test** all the people of earth.

To *try* means "to test or scrutinize." The time of testing, scrutinizing, and putting to proof is directed at churches that belong to Jesus. All churches are tested; the exceptions are the church of Philadelphia and portions of Sardis and Thyatira. Those three do not need to be scrutinized/tested under pressure. Those have grown into maturity in Christ; He approves of them.

Jesus told them to hold fast and not have their crown taken. That crown is the type given to overcomers—a "victor's crown." Those have proven their faith; they are to be **steadfast** in victory until He returns.

The two differing types of crowns cited in Revelation are addressed in a future chapter. The Philadelphia church receives the crown of victory—not authority.

THE CHURCH OF LAODICEA

Revelation 3:15-20, *"I know thy works, that thou art neither cold nor hot: I would thou wast cold or hot. So then because thou art lukewarm, and neither cold nor hot, I will spew thee out of my mouth. Because thou sayest, I am rich, and increased with goods, and have need of nothing; and*

38

knowest not that thou art wretched, and miserable, and poor, and blind, and naked: I counsel thee to buy of me gold tried in the fire, that thou mayest be rich; and white raiment, that thou mayest be clothed, and that the shame of thy nakedness do not appear; and anoint thine eyes with eye salve, that thou mayest see. As many as I love, I rebuke and chasten: be zealous therefore, and repent. Behold, I stand at the door, and knock: if any man hear my voice, and open the door, I will come in to him, and will sup with him, and he will with me."

The church of Laodicea is "a-middle-of-the-road" church. Great compromise remains between the godliness Scripture demands and the normal Laodicean lifestyle. Those living this lifestyle surmise they are doing well. Spiritually, they are saved; materially, they do not have any needs. Jesus rebukes them, telling them they are neither hot nor cold; their "indifferent" attitude toward Him is sickening. He counsels to use some physical wealth to do spiritual works; then they would possess "true" wealth. In 1 Corinthians 3:11-13, the works that Christians can perform are either "wood, hay and stubble" or "gold, silver and precious stones." The Laodiceans obviously did the prior—failing to serve God with a heartfelt desire.

The same "semi-religious" attitude is in their spiritual/personal relationship with God. Jesus gave a similar warning in Matthew.

Matthew 7:21-23, *"Not every one that saith unto me, Lord, Lord, shall enter into the kingdom of heaven; but he that doeth the will of my Father which is in heaven. **Many** will say to me in that day, Lord, Lord, have we not prophesied in thy name? and in thy name have cast out devils? and **in thy*** *name done many wonderful works? And then will I profess unto them, I never knew you: depart from me, ye that work iniquity."*

It is possible to look like a Christian to others, but God looks at motives. 1 Samuel 16:7 says, *"...for man looketh on the outward appearance, but the LORD looketh on the heart."*

The Laodiceans are **loved**; Jesus **rebukes and chastens those He loves** and calls them to repentance. **If** they repent, they open the door to allow Jesus to be their "author and finisher of faith." Previously, these were called by His name but have not known Him personally. **They** have a choice to make; **they** must open the door. God does not force His way into relationship.

Many people do not like to hear about the Laodicean church; those believers did not please God. Realize there is **great hope** because of them; they did everything **wrong** in the beginning of their faith—both in their physical lives and spiritual relationship. Yet, with repentance, there is hope! That good news should encourage everyone.

Jesus has made corrections with clarity and rebuke to the Laodiceans and other churches. Chastisement is addressed by His Word. It is certain that churches failing to teach God's chastisement, are not presenting **complete** scriptural truth. The love of Jesus needs to be taught and cannot be ignored, but there must be a balance of scriptural principles. Biblical precepts include His loving compassion, and correction through chastening.

When chastening from God was **not** exhibited or taught by leadership, His people wandered into **great** error.

*"I have seen also in the prophets of Jerusalem a horrible thing: they commit adultery, and walk in lies: **they strengthen also the hands of evildoers, that none doth***

40

return from his wickedness [repent]: *they are all of them unto me as Sodom, and the inhabitants thereof as Gomorrah"* (Jeremiah 23:14).

Those were the people of God, but they lost regard for His Word. The ones leading them were living and teaching error.

> *"And ye have forgotten the exhortation which speaketh unto you as unto children, My son,* **despise not** *thou the* **chastening** *of the Lord, nor faint* **when thou art rebuked** *of him: For whom the Lord* **loveth** *he* **chasteneth**, *and scourgeth* **every son** *whom he* **receiveth**. *If ye endure chastening, God dealeth with you as with sons; for* **what son** *is he whom the* **father chastenth not**? *But* **if ye** *be* **without** *chastisement,* **whereof all are partakers**, *then are ye bastards, and* **not sons"** (Hebrews 12:5-8).

How long is it since the Lord rebuked or chastised you? If He hasn't lately, you are either walking in maturity as "Philadelphia," or He is not treating you as a beloved child. Sincerely ask if you belong to Him, or possibly have ignored Him. Only the Holy Spirit is able to identify where you are in your walk with Christ. Have the courage to ask Him.

* * * * *

Thus far, no comments were offered about the "rewards" given to those who repent and overcome. All seven churches **share** in all "overcomers" rewards. One church doesn't receive one reward and another church another reward. *"To him that overcometh…"* is the **common** theme for those **receiving rewards**. When Jesus is finished correcting the seven churches, only

41

two groups of Christians remain: 1) those who overcome, and 2) those who do not. The rewards given to **overcomers** are as follows:

Ephesus — *"to eat of the tree of life"* (2:7)

Smyrna — *"a crown of life; shall not be hurt of the second death"* (2:10, 11)

Pergamos — *"eat of the hidden manna; give him a white stone, and in the stone a new name written"* (2:17)

Thyatira — *"power over the nations; the morning star"* (2:26, 28)

Sardis — *"clothed in white raiment; will not blot out his name of the book of life; I will confess his name before my Father"* (3:4, 5)

Philadelphia — *"will I make a pillar in the temple of my God; I will write upon him the name of my God, and the name of the city of my God; I will write upon him my new name"* (3:12)

Laodicea — *"will I grant to sit with me in my throne, even as I also overcame"* (3:21)

Looking at the rewards cumulatively indicates a compound collection dispersed to all overcoming believers. If any divisions are to be made, it would be for **when** they are distributed. For instance, *"eating from the tree of life"* occurs after the millennial reign of Christ and during the era of New Jerusalem. The *"crown of life"* is likely to be allocated at the Great White Throne Judgment because believers *"shall not be hurt of the second death."* To *"eat of the hidden manna and have a new name that no one knows"* is a means to receive provision needed while the Antichrist rules earth. To *"have power over the nations"* is reserved for the millennial reign of Christ. To be *"clothed in white"* likely applies during the tribulation and wrath **before** Christ returns. To *"sit with Jesus in His throne"* will occur during His millennial reign.

Looking at the bestowed rewards in this manner indicates **all** rewards are for **all** overcomers. The seven churches addressed in Revelation are the ones existing at the end of the Church Age. They are not meant to apply for diverse time periods throughout history.

Obviously, not everyone corrected by Jesus repents. There are those such as Jezebel (Revelation 2:22), going into great tribulation (great pressure). Never the less, **Jesus has not given up on them**! Correction was given to spare them the coming hardship (pressure of tribulation). Upcoming passages in Revelation portray that group.

CHAPTER 4

This chapter of Revelation contains a superb description for being close to God. To receive the "word picture," please read all eleven verses.

Exhibiting worship, living creatures say, *"...Holy, holy, holy, LORD God Almighty, which was, and is, and is to come"* (v. 8). Twenty-four elders fall down and cast crowns before God's throne. A Christian praise chorus was written to that theme: "We fall down / We lay our crowns / At the feet of Jesus." A deeper meaning for that gesture is discovered through comprehending the crown types distinguished by Scripture.

The *crowns* of the elders (Greek: *stephanos*) are "a twine or a wreath." That chaplet was used as a symbol of honor, a prize in public games. Those crowns are the award of victory. The elders have cast crowns of "victory" back to God, thereby declaring **God** is the One worthy of recognition. They realize God's grace motivated them so they **return victory honor** back to God in worship.

Other crowns (Greek: *diadema*) establishing authority and rule are worn by kings. Jesus wears crowns of authority when He returns (Revelation 19:12). There is a distinction between the "overcoming crown" of the elder and the "ruling crown" of authority. Overcoming believers receive the caplet of victory.

* * * * *

Notice the heavenly worship and words utilized by the elders: God is **worthy** to receive **glory, honor and power**. This example is not **about** God, but words directed **to** Him. Honoring God as the elders and living creatures is also for human application.

The reason of God's worth is a point of interest. Verse 11 states, *"...for thou hast created all things."* The reason God is worthy to receive worship is because **He is the Creator**. Evolution is a weapon of Satan fashioned against God and the people He wants to save; that theory is an effective way to **steal faith** from mankind and **thieve** worship from God.

It makes sense that God's adversary would attempt deception through posing an idea like evolution. People had a sense of creation until evolution was introduced. Romans 1:19, 20, state that creation itself is the evidence for man that God exists; therefore, man is without excuse when he denies God.

Evolution steals faith and worship by introducing a theory based on human intellect. Reasoning produces thoughts denying creation. Even believers may begin pondering the possibility, trying to combine creation and evolution; that attitude is a compromise of God's Word. Compromise in one area opens the door for further doubt. Darwin's theory is a powerful weapon for Satan.

Read and believe your Bible; it is a strong defense the Holy Spirit uses for protection from the influences of evolution.

CHAPTER 5

According to Revelation 5, there is activity in heaven. Jesus is the only One worthy to open the seals of a scroll. Opening those seals brings about cataclysmic events which **generate** the **end** of the Church Age.

In the "Lord's Prayer," Jesus taught believers to petition the Father, *"Thy kingdom come, Thy will be done in earth, as it is in heaven"* (Matthew 6:10). Peace on earth (the will of the Father) will only occur when Jesus rules it. The "Lord's Prayer" essentially urges believers to pray for the opening of the seals; it is the only way the contents of the scroll, the "kingdom of God" can be established. Earth must **experience** the seven seals **before** the scroll can be opened. Opening the scroll launches the coming physical kingdom, the millennial reign of Jesus. It is why John *"...wept much..."* (v. 4) when no one could open it. There could **never** be godliness on earth without opening the scroll.

In Revelation 5:6, Jesus is portrayed as a slain lamb having seven horns. A later chapter reveals that the horns used in Revelation represent ruling authorities. For Jesus the Lamb, they signify the seven churches.

Then this passage says His seven eyes represent seven spirits of God. Additional Scripture creates clarity for that verse. Zechariah 4:10 indicates the eyes of the Lord see **everything**, *"...with those seven; they are the eyes of the LORD, which run to and fro through the whole earth."* Jesus knows everything happening on earth through those seven eyes; nothing is hidden.

The number "7" is regarded as "the number of completion." The Lord sees completely through seven spirits giving Him complete vision, and nothing is concealed.

The seven spirits of God are not the One and only Holy

Spirit. The Holy Spirit has personality and thoughts of His own—not simply eyes that see everything.

Verse 12 reveals worship; humans can learn how to worship via this heavenly example *"...power, and riches, and wisdom, and strength, and honor, and glory, and blessing"* are more words presenting adoration directly to God. Chapter 5 reveals heavenly worship, as did chapter 4. Every believer can worship God by replicating what occurs in heaven. Hopefully, everyone will learn from the heavenly examples of worship while focusing on God.

The Seals

In an earlier chapter some *keys* were mentioned. From this point, those keys will be implemented. **Events** are pursued, as opposed to chronological chapter occurrences.

Something pertinent happens in Revelation 6:1, which says, *"And I saw when the Lamb opened **one** of the seals...."* Jesus started to open the seals depicting the end-time. A close examination of the wording of this verse reveals a key. It sets precedent; the key is the word "one." That cardinal number is not to be overlooked; it clarifies **order** (or lack of) for all seven seals.

If five gifts were placed on a tabletop, then someone were invited into the room, and someone said to that person, "All the gifts are for you; go ahead and open them," which gift would the person choose first? Would he **start** with the first gift to the right or to the left? Would he choose one from the middle? After all, he has five from which to **choose**. According to the Greek wording, that illustration presents the situation taking place in Revelation 6:1.

Jesus opens **one** of the seals—not necessarily the **"first"** seal of the scroll, though it **could** be. The condition is the same as the person's receiving gifts. He will choose **one** of the five to open **first**. (Note: many modern English translations say "first" seal believing the word *first* produced proper English understanding. The Greek manuscripts say "one.")

The *first* seal Jesus opened is conveyed by the *cardinal number* "one." A **cardinal** number communicates **quantity**.

If Jesus opened the *first* seal, He would have set **order** to the seals by using the *ordinal number* "first." The ordinal or cardinal number establishes the meaning as to whether **chronology** or **quantity** is expressed.

Because Jesus used a *cardinal number*, He was revealing the

quantity as each seal opened. He displays events that occur during each "one" of the seals. Revelation is silent pertaining to chronology. That concept is important to grasp! Attempting to put the seals into chronological order requires additional Scriptures. The Gospels are the best place to perceive an order for the end-time events.

In Matthew 24:3-14, Jesus pictured a complete **overview** of the end-time. That particular passage contains the **basic events** in **order**, minus other details. After listing the basic events, Jesus said, *"...and **then** shall the end come"* (Matthew 24:14). The seven seals of Revelation also give a complete overview of the end-time. Harmony between that gospel passage and the Revelation seals needs to be established.

THE FIRST SEAL

Revelation 6:2, *"And I saw, and behold a white horse: and he that sat upon him had a bow; and a crown was given unto him: and he went forth conquering, and to conquer."* The rider of that horse wears a crown (diadem) signifying authority. The white horse denotes someone victorious. The passage does not say the rider's "conquering" produced physical death as would be assumed when people are conquered.

Opening the **second** seal reveals **physical** death. The conquering in the first seal must be of a spiritual nature—not producing physical death. The rider is carrying a bow. How can a bow be used as a weapon without arrows? A bow is a *bend*; it represents God's Truth that has been "bent" and twisted by false teaching. The rider's spiritual conquering is accomplished by causing people to be deceived; in so doing, **Truth** is conquered.

Some believe the white horse means Jesus must be the rider. Jesus will ride a white horse to signify victory, but He will not be carrying a bow; He will carry a **straight** scepter (Hebrews 1:8); it represents unbent Truth and righteousness—not a bow of deceit.

Is anything Jesus said in the Gospel of Matthew relevant to the first seal of Revelation? Yes. When questioned by His disciples concerning the end of the world, Jesus' **first** response was, *"Take heed that no man **deceive you**. For many shall come in my name, saying, I am Christ and shall **deceive many**"* (Matthew 24:4, 5).

"Christ" is not the last name of Jesus. Prior to beginning His earthly ministry, He was known as "Jesus, son of Joseph" or "Jesus of Nazareth." When He **began ministry** through teaching and doing miracles, He became known as Jesus **the** "Christ." In Greek, "the Christ" and in the Hebrew "the Messiah" both mean "Anointed One." According to the vernacular of Jesus' time, any anointed leader fulfills the qualification to be a "Christ"—one who is "consecrated" by God.

Jesus taught that many will come in His name. They are Christian leaders. They claim they are *christs* (anointed to lead). Many anointed teachers will rise up. Jesus said *"Take heed that no man deceive you."* They will not teach complete truth. (Think about all the errors Jesus addressed in the seven churches.)

Those *christs* are the **same** as the end-time **false teachers** Paul said would **infiltrate** the church (2 Timothy 4:3, 4). They teach false doctrine. **Jesus and Paul** said the **same** thing. In the end-time, some church leaders will teach false doctrine. Agreement between 2 Timothy and Matthew establishes a biblical end-time theme; it is verified in both. The truth will be twisted **within** the Christian faith by anointed leadership.

Can that theme be found in Revelation? Yes, it is perceived in the first seal. Matthew and 2 Timothy **agree** concerning false teachers and thereby agree with the above concept for the rider of the white horse carrying a bow. The end-time begins with Christian teachers presenting false doctrines. Those passages provide a solid, biblical foundation for the first seal of Revelation, producing unity in these Scriptures.

Jesus was not referring to other religions in Matthew. False religions have plagued God's people from the beginnings of biblical faith. These end-time false ones are **within** the gatherings of the faithful; believers are to *"take heed"* **not** to be **deceived**.

Indeed, truth has been "conquered" **within** Christianity's households; false teachings abound. Anointed leaders have allowed truth to become bent. Think of some of the peripheral movements that emerged and emphasized extreme doctrines in recent years; "positive thinking," "prosperity gospel," and "faith name-it-and-claim-it" theologies are examples. These teachings should have been minimal at best, never developing into the **focus** of major doctrines. Many "seeker-friendly" churches center on a "love" gospel, never using the word *repent* to deal with sin. Add to the above list all the errors in doctrine Jesus corrected in addressing the "seven churches." False doctrines within Christianity are numerous; the scriptural prophesies concerning them are fulfilled.

The atonement of the cross of Jesus followed by the reign of the Holy Spirit is "straight" truth. A focus on the kingdom of God (the rule by God that Jesus said He was sent to teach [Luke 4:43]) should have been emphasized. It is carried out by the Holy Spirit working in the conscience. (These will be addressed in later chapters.) Jesus' words have been proven true: **many have been deceived**. The rider of the white horse has been conquering Truth and **continues** to conquer in this generation. Obviously, Jesus **opened the first seal** decades ago.

THE SECOND SEAL

Revelation 6:3, 4, *"And when he had opened the second seal, I heard the second beast say, Come, and see. And there went out another horse that was red: and power was given to him that sat thereon to take peace from the earth, and that*

51

they should kill one another: and there was given unto him a great sword. "

Physical death accompanies the rider of the red horse.

After Jesus addressed the false teachers in Matthew 24:5, He noted another matter in verse 6: *"And ye shall hear of wars and rumors of wars: see that ye be not troubled: for all these things must come to pass, but the end is not yet. "* Listening to daily news reports from year to year verifies the world is full of wars and unrest. The words of Jesus are proven true. He was foretelling the season of wars being observed in current events. Those *"wars and rumors of wars"* are **not immediate** to the end; they are a precursor to the end. Jesus said, *"...the end is not yet."* He said the people will **hear** of wars; hearing of them is made possible via the **modern media** of this present generation.

The second seal of Revelation lines up with "wars and rumors of wars" in Matthew 24:6. Jesus is currently **opening the second seal**.

THE THIRD SEAL

Revelation 6:5, 6, *"And when he had opened the third seal, I heard the third beast say, Come and see. And I beheld, and lo a black horse; and he that sat on him had a pair of balances in his hand. And I heard a voice in the midst of the four beasts say, A measure of wheat for a penny, and three measures of barley for a penny; and see thou hurt not the oil and the wine. "*

At the opening of the third seal, the rider of the black horse manipulates the food staples of earth. What is next in Matthew? Immediately following fighting, the next event noted is *"famines. "* Matthew 24:7, *"For nation shall rise against nation, and kingdom against kingdom: and there shall be famines....*" In Matthew, after the wars and feuding, famines occur; that bonds together with Revelation's rider of the black horse affecting food quantities. In Matthew, Jesus noted along with famines there would be pestilences (diseases) and earthquakes.

Today, instances of those dreadful events are escalating. The second seal i.e., the current era is a time of "wars." As the second seal's wars escalate, conditions are prepared for the closely following third seal; it opens during the wars of the second. After the time of feuding (the second seal), the third seal begins food shortages, diseases and earthquakes.

A voice spoke out of the midst of the four beasts and told the rider of the black horse, *"...see thou hurt not the oil and the wine"* (Revelation 6:6). This Scripture needs to be considered. Additional Scriptures will indicate this phrase is given in reference to the "overcoming" church. For that reason, the third seal is **very** significant. The believer's prayer for deliverance in Luke 21:36 and Zephaniah 2:3 will be awarded after the third seal is opened.

Why does verse 6 correlate to the "overcomers"? In Christian faith, the oil and wine are basic elements. Oil is used as anointing oil for both consecration and healing. The wine is a major part of the communion supper. In Revelation 6:6, God is saying, "Though famine is coming in troubled times, the people of the oil and the wine (overcoming Christians) are not to be harmed."

Other end-time Scriptures confirm God's intent to care for those serving Him, while the disobedient and unbelieving suffer great hardship. Isaiah 65:13 and 14 tell us:

"Therefore thus saith the Lord GOD, Behold, my servants shall eat, but ye shall be hungry: behold, my servants shall drink, but ye shall be thirsty: behold, my servants shall rejoice, but ye shall be ashamed: Behold, my servants shall

53

sing for joy of heart, but ye shall cry for sorrow of heart, and shall howl for vexation of spirit."

That passage definitely applies during the end-time; the context of Isaiah 65:17 cites the creation of the **new** heavens and earth. The new heavens and earth are in Revelation 21:1, proving both Scriptures pertain to the same era.

Isaiah 65:8 (the same end-time passage), reveals that God uses the metaphoric word "wine" to **represent His servants**; the reference to **wine** in Revelation 6:6 is **biblically** a metaphor used to identify God's servants. *"Thus saith the LORD, As the new **wine** is found in the cluster* [overcomers], *and one saith, **Destroy it not*** [the angel of Revelation 7:2, 3]; *for a blessing is in it: so will I do for **my servants' sakes**, that **I may not destroy them all*** [the sealed overcomers]." (That theme will be expounded soon.)

Identical end-time relationship between Isaiah and Revelation occurs again; both books depict the same event. In Isaiah 27:1, there is a time when God punishes leviathan (Satan). That event is also revealed by Revelation 20:1-3; proving Isaiah 27 applies in the end-time.

In Isaiah 27, the Lord again utilizes the "wine" metaphor for His servants. They are grouped together in *"a **vineyard** of red **wine**."* The concept of grouping overcoming believers together will be elaborated on later.

*"In that day the LORD with his sore and great and strong sword shall punish leviathan the piercing serpent, even leviathan that crooked serpent; and he shall slay the dragon that is in the sea. In that day sing ye unto her, A vineyard of red **wine. I the LORD do keep it**; I will water it every moment: **lest any hurt it**, I will keep it night and day"* (Isaiah 27:1-3).

54

The Scripture reveals people under divine protection while God deals with Satan (leviathan). The end-time metaphors to "wine" are found in Isaiah 27:1-3, 65:8 and Revelation 6:6. One of the rewards for overcomers is they will *"...eat of the hidden manna"* (Revelation 2:17). These passages substantiate **provision** is allocated to God's servants during the end-time.

* * * * *

Continuing with the third seal requires moving ahead in Revelation. An event occurring **during** the third seal is described in another passage.

> Revelation 7:1-3, *"And after these things I saw four angels standing on the four corners of the earth, holding the four winds of the earth, that the wind should not blow on the earth, nor on the sea, nor on any tree. And I saw another angel ascending from the east, having the seal of the living God: and he cried with a loud voice to the four angels, to whom it was given to **hurt** the earth and the sea, Saying, **Hurt not** the earth, neither the sea, nor the trees, **till we have sealed** the servants of our God in their foreheads."*

Verses 2 and 3 state the earth and sea are **not** to be harmed **until** the servants of God are **sealed** (provided for). **Hurting** the earth will cause the famine mentioned in Revelation 6:6. The oil and wine (overcoming Christians) are **not** to be **hurt**; Isaiah said God's servants will eat and drink while others hunger and thirst (Isaiah 65:13, 14).

During the third seal, the overcoming church is set apart and provided for by God! The angels are **not** allowed to **hurt** the earth until the servants of God are sealed. The voice in Revelation 6:6 said, *"...see thou hurt not the oil and the wine."* That is why the third seal is very significant to the overcoming church.

THE FOURTH SEAL

Revelation 6:7, 8, *"And when he had opened the fourth seal, I heard the voice of the fourth beast say, Come and see. And I looked, and behold a pale horse: and his name that sat on him was Death, and Hell followed with him. And power was given unto them over the fourth part of the earth, to kill with sword, and with hunger, and with death, and with the beasts of the earth."*

When the fourth seal is opened, there is massive loss of human life. The third seal initiated food shortages which escalate into famines. In the fourth seal those famines produce starvation. The wars originating from the second seal continue escalating, now producing huge losses of life. The fourth seal encompasses weapons, starvation, beasts of earth, and people simply dying (plagues?). One quarter of earth's population will be destroyed. If death and hell are following, the future for those **not** under divine protection is revealed. The ones protected by God are sealed and provided for.

All of this upheaval is pictured by the riders of the black and pale horses. **Both** riders from Revelation are addressed in Matthew 24:7; the Revelation seals are following the gospel's sequence of events.

THE FIFTH SEAL

"And when he had opened the fifth seal, I saw under the altar the souls of them that were slain for the word of God, and for the testimony which they held: And they cried with a loud voice, saying, How long, O Lord, holy and true, dost

56

thou not judge and avenge our blood on them that dwell on the earth? And white robes were given unto every one of them; and it was said unto them, that they should rest yet for a little season, until their fellow servants also and their brethren, that should be killed as they were, should be fulfilled" (Revelation 6:9-11).

At the opening of the fifth seal, John sees martyrs waiting for God's judgment to begin against the wicked. They are told to wait until other believers are martyred during the tribulation. Think about that answer. God begins to "judge and avenge blood" (His wrath) **after** future martyrs are **killed**. Their predecessors *"under the altar"* and *"slain for the word of God"* are **waiting** for them.

The cloaked chronology reveals the timing for God's **judgment and vengeance upon the wicked**. His wrath is launched by means of trumpet and vial judgments **after** all tribulation martyrs have been killed. His response to the question of verse 10, *"...how long...dost **thou not judge**..."* is answered in verse 11: *"...**until their fellow servants** also and their brethren, that **should also be killed** as they were...."* Only then will God's judgment begin on the wicked.

The same timing is also expressed by 2 Corinthians 10:6, which says, *"And having in a readiness to **revenge** all **disobedience**, when **your obedience is fulfilled**."* Once all of the church has demonstrated obedience, God takes vengeance on all the disobedient. These passages confirm the same timing.

The number of martyrs will be vast. When Jesus spoke to the seven churches, He approved of some **because they obeyed** and did not need any correction, namely Philadelphia. Others become overcomers because they heed correction and **repent**. Those not repenting go into tribulation. Their only entrance into heaven is by **their choice to be obedient unto death**. After the time for killing martyrs is **completed**, God's judgment begins upon the wicked.

An additional Scripture verifies the same sequence; judgment will **first** begin in the house of God, 1 Peter 4:17, *"For the time is come that judgment must **begin** at the house of God: and if it **first** begin at **us**, what shall the **end** be of them that **obey not** the gospel of God?"* God deals with His people first and then the wicked. The Scriptures agree.

Matthew 24:9 relates to the fifth-seal martyrs, *"Then shall they deliver you up to be afflicted, and shall kill you: and ye shall be hated of all nations for my name's sake."* The Christians are hated and killed (martyred) for His name's sake. Matthew 24:9 and Revelation's fifth seal continue following the same sequence; they teach order for the same event and confirm one another. A curve is coming on this road.

THE SIXTH SEAL AND SEVENTH SEAL

Revelation 6:12-17, *"And I beheld when he had opened the sixth seal, and, lo, there was a great earthquake; and the **sun became black** as sackcloth of hair, and the **moon became as blood**; And the **stars of heaven fell** unto the earth, even as a fig tree casteth her untimely figs, when she is shaken of a mighty wind. And the **heaven departed as a scroll** when it is rolled together; and every mountain and island were moved out of their places. And the **kings of the earth, and the great men, and the rich men, and the chief captains, and the mighty men, and every bondman, and every free man**, hid themselves in the dens and in the rocks of the mountains; And said to the mountains and rocks, Fall upon us, and **hide us from the face of him** that sitteth on the throne, and from the **wrath of the Lamb**: For the great **day** of his **wrath is come**; and who shall be able to stand?"*

58

The sixth seal depicts **Jesus' return**; it is the **culmination** of **wrath** upon the ungodly. This passage describes the very **end**—the **last day** of wrath. This "day of the Lord" is the end of normal world history. Jesus overcomes all powers of earth and begins a one-thousand-year era when He is the supreme authority.

The Gospel of Matthew describes the same final day:

> *"Immediately **after** the **tribulation** of those days** shall the **sun be darkened**, and the **moon shall not give her light**, and the **stars shall fall from heaven**, and the **powers of the heavens shall be shaken**: And then shall appear the sign of the Son of man in heaven: and then shall **all the tribes of the earth mourn**, and **they shall see the Son of man coming** in the clouds of heaven with power and great glory"* (Matthew 24:29, 30).

Comparing the bolded words from both passages shows the phenomena are the same; they are descriptions of the same occurrence. **Jesus returns** to rule and reign; that is the **final** event encompassed by the seals and Gospels.

A problem presents itself in Revelation; a seventh seal remains unopened. "Wrath judgments" via angels were not distributed. (Wrath in the form of seven judgments is dispensed by angels; later, a final day of wrath is dispensed by Jesus at His return.) The **seventh** seal brings seven wrath judgments upon the wicked. Those judgments must be fulfilled **before** the final day of wrath. (Keep the illustration of a person's opening gifts in mind.) At this point, it is obvious Jesus opened the seal describing "**His return**," **before** He opened the seal portraying "**seven judgments of wrath**." The **seventh** seal contains wrath judgments occurring **before** the "return of Christ" in the **sixth** seal.

When Jesus used a cardinal instead of an ordinal number for

the "first" seal He opened, He did **not** establish chronological order for the seals; He established *quantity*. He could **choose** to reveal the contents of **any seal** at **any time**. The sixth (His return) and the seventh (wrath judgments) are opened by Him in reverse chronological order.

The contents of the seventh seal are revealed over the course of three chapters (8 through 10). That portion of John's vision has more detail disclosed than any other. At the **conclusion** of the seventh seal, **during** the **last** wrath judgment, the sixth seal is opened. The millennial reign of Jesus begins, bringing an end to the era called the Church Age.

The seven seals and Matthew 24:3-14 give an overview of aspects included in the end-time era.

 The Doubled Prophecy of the "Kine-and-Corn Key" is used from this point.

The events occurring from this locale forward are listed together in parallel passages. The "kine and corn" were interpreted by Joseph. *"And for that the dream was doubled unto Pharaoh twice; it is because the thing is established by God, and God will shortly bring it to pass"* (Genesis 41:32). This book uses Bible-given prophetic understanding while interpreting a prophetic book—Revelation. Remember, *kine* and *corn* are not identically the same, neither are John's visions. The general themes of the visions with specific common subjects tie them together.

Another key referred to is perspective (location and viewpoint) of John as he watched events occur. He wrote what he saw from his viewing "position"; then he gave descriptions according to his vocabulary.

Synonymous words are keys that unite passages. Multiple passages offer additional information.

GOD'S DIVINE PROTECTION

"And after these things I saw **four angels standing on the four corners of the earth**, *holding the four winds of the earth, that the wind should not blow on the earth, nor on the sea, nor on any tree. And I saw* **another angel ascending from the east**, *having the* **seal** *of the living God: and he cried with a loud voice to the four angels to whom it was given to* **hurt** *the earth and the sea"* (Revelation 7:1, 2).

In this vision, John saw angels standing on the four corners of earth, holding the winds. He watched another angel **come up** from the east to talk to those holding the winds. He saw angels stationed around the globe. Where is John's location that enables him to describe the positions of the five angels? His perspective is from "outer space," i.e., gazing down at earth. He is **looking down** at the **globe** to see all four angels holding the winds and another angel **ascending** from the east. **Space** is the only vantage point capable of allowing John to observe all five angels.

Later, it is critical to consider his position while he describes another significant event from that same vantage point. Being **located** in space influences the wording he employs.

What would be some natural consequences when angels hold the winds in order to **hurt** the earth and sea? One of the first effects is the absence of rain. Having no wind would also hinder cross-pollination of vegetation. The combination of those two would result in crop failures. Literally or metaphorically, the angels' hurting the earth will produce worldwide **famine**. That famine fulfills prophecies contained in the **third** seal (Revelation 6:6), Matthew 24:7 and Isaiah 65:13, 14.

In Revelation 7:3, servants of God are sealed in their

foreheads **before** the earth is **hurt**. Isaiah 65:13 verifies God provides for His people in the end-time while others hunger and thirst. In Revelation, rewards are listed for those who overcome; they eat of **hidden** manna. In Zephaniah 2:3, some believers are *"hid."* A plan of God is revealed by these Scriptures.

Isaiah 65:8, said, *"Thus saith the LORD, As the new **wine** [God's servants] is **found in the cluster**, and one saith, **Destroy it not**; for a blessing is in it: so will I do for **my servants' sakes**, that **I may not destroy them all.** "* The phrase, "found in a cluster" fits together and agrees with New Testament Scripture. It applies when "overcomers" are grouped together. Jesus describes this occurrence by referring to "eagles" gathering at a carcass (forthcoming study). In both passages, the theme is an assembling together for provision in order to avoid destruction. God truly has a plan to protect His overcoming servants.

> *"Come, my people, enter thou into thy chambers, and shut thy doors about thee: **hide** thyself as it were for a little moment, until the **indignation** be overpast. For, behold, the LORD cometh out of his place **to punish the inhabitants of the earth** for their iniquity: the earth also shall disclose her blood, and shall no more cover her slain"* (Isaiah 26:20, 21).

The Hebrew word for *indignation* means "fury, God's displeasure with sin." His servants **hide** as God's fury against sin passes by. His anger is unleashed in the seven angelically dispensed wrath judgments (upcoming study). The era for **hiding** is when all the inhabitants of earth are to be punished, i.e., the end-time. The end-time era for this passage is certain; it is **verified** because the **resurrection** of the dead is addressed one verse prior, *"Thy dead men shall live, together with my **dead body shall they arise**. **Awake and sing, ye that dwell in dust**: for thy dew is as the dew of herbs,* *and the earth shall **cast out the dead*** (Isaiah 26:19). The resurrection of the dead is at the Great White Throne Judgment in Revelation 20:11-15. Isaiah 26:19 is definitely an Old Testament, end-time passage; thereby verses 20 and 21 are also. The unity of the Old and New Testament presents a solid foundation; they delineate hiding and special provision for believers during the end-time. (Note: the above resurrection is not for the saints meeting Jesus in the air at His return; that resurrection and rapture will be studied later.)

 ## The Sealing of 144,000

In Revelation 7:3, a group of God's servants are sealed in their foreheads. Then John said, *"And I heard the number of them which were sealed: and there were sealed a hundred and forty and four thousand of all the tribes of the children of Israel"* (v. 4). That "sealing" has been applied and explained in various ways by others. Each student of the Bible has likely formed his opinion and may not readily agree with what is presented here. Please patiently read through this entire presented interpretation.

When John observed events in the beginning of chapter 7, he was in space looking down at earth. From there he watched as twelve groups of twelve thousand were sealed. The description of those groups was referenced by the names of the twelve tribes of Israel as recorded in Revelation 7:5-8. Were the ones sealed, Israelites?

In Numbers 2:1-34 a "pattern" was used to organize the children of Israel around the tabernacle. God instructed Moses to always use that pattern every time the nation camped. The center of the following diagram represents the Tabernacle, although it was not round. This drawing represents an aerial view—the same perspective John received in space as he watched twelve groups of twelve thousand sealed by angels.

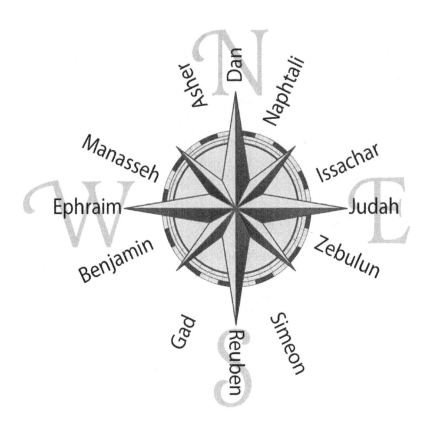

From **space** and being an Israelite, John described what he saw by what he was familiar with. **Hebrew** history gave him his only resource to communicate what he viewed. His ancestors, the twelve tribes of Israel, assembled to and dispersed from around the tabernacle to the north, south, east, and west. Looking down at the globe was unique; he had never seen a photograph of the earth from space. **His location** for the vision explains how the **overcoming church** from around the world is represented by 144,000 sealed and referred to as Israelites. **Overcomers** from around the world are the ones sealed.

Realize that **Revelation is written to Christians**—not to Jews. John described what he saw using **his** vocabulary and knowledge to describe the visions.

That group of overcoming believers is divinely protected from the catastrophes that affect all other people on earth. Zephaniah 2:3, "…*it may be ye shall be **hid** in the day of the LORD's anger."* God divinely **hides** the sealed **before** His **wrath** is unleashed. Isaiah 26:20, 21, state that the people of God *hide* until the fury of God is accomplished. God punishes the inhabitants of earth for their wickedness while His servants are hidden.

A closer examination of the 144,000 requires using the prophetic key of doubled prophecy. **Overcomers** from the seven churches have the Father's name written on them (Revelation 3:12). The 144,000 and overcomers from the seven churches are the same group, both have God's name written on them. The 144,000 are shown to John again at the beginning of his second vision.

 Revelation 14:1-5, *"And I looked, and, lo, a Lamb stood on the mount Zion, and with him a **hundred forty and four thousand**, having his **Father's name written in their foreheads**. And I heard a voice from heaven, as the voice of many waters, and as the voice of a great thunder: and I heard the voice of harpers harping with their harps: And they sung as it were a new song before the throne, and before the four beasts, and the elders: and no man could learn that song but the hundred and forty and four thousand, which were redeemed from the earth. These are they which were not defiled with women; for they are virgins. These are they which **follow the Lamb whithersoever he goeth**. These were **redeemed** from among men, being the **firstfruits** unto God and to the Lamb. And in their mouth was found **no guile**: for they are without fault before the throne of God."*

In both passages (Revelation 7:4 and Revelation 14:1-5) a

65

group of people numbering 144,000 have a "seal" **or** "God's name" **in** their **foreheads**. The "**overcoming**" church has the name of God **written in** their **foreheads** (Revelation 3:12). Revelation 14:1-5 is a different view of Revelation 7:3-8; it is a doubled prophetic vision. John saw the same believers in two separate visions.

These 144,000 "follow the **Lamb** wherever He goes." The twelve tribes sealed in chapter 7 cannot be unbelieving Jews. To re-emphasize, unbelieving Jews do not recognize Jesus as their Savior/Lamb; they will not follow Him. The sealed are not physically Israelites; they are spiritually.

Revelation 14:4 states that those in this group are "virgins" and "not defiled with women." The use of the word *virgins* is metaphorical; God referred to His **disobedient** people in Ezekiel 23:1-4, as the **whores** Aholah and Aholibah. After **they returned** to **Him**, He metaphorically referred to **His people** as *virgins* (Jeremiah 31:4). Paul also used that same metaphor: *"...that I may present you* [the church] *as a chaste **virgin** to Christ"* (2 Corinthians 11:2).

Revelation 14 describes a group of people who resist the temptations of the world and discipline themselves to live by God's standard. They are "without fault" before Him (v. 5). They have overcome by their obedience. God metaphorically calls them virgins; they are those from the "seven churches" who have **overcome**, *"That he might present it to himself a glorious church, not having spot, or wrinkle, or any such thing; but that it should be holy and without blemish"* (Ephesians 5:27). Such is the description of the church that Jesus raises up and then returns for.

Those believers are still on earth (v. 2). John heard a voice **from** heaven, and waters, thunders and harpers (v. 3). He heard them **sing** a new song **from** heaven (the heavenly beasts and elders). No **man** could learn the **song** except the 144,000 (v. 3); they were still on earth. Think again about Isaiah 65:13, 14 (God's end-time servants); the passage records God's servants eating, drinking, rejoicing and **singing**. The servants provided for and singing in Isaiah, are the 144,000 first-fruits in Revelation 14:1-5. They are the only humans allowed to sing the song heard from heaven (Revelation 14:3).

Is the number 144,000 literal? It can be but doesn't have to be. The numbering system by biblical precedence was for males twenty years of age and older. That principle carried over from the Old and into the New Testament; it is illustrated in Matthew 14:21. The Bible **excludes** the number of women and children who were present, only recording the five thousand men who had eaten. The 144,000 should be adult males; women and children are not numbered. There is no explanation of how that number could represent a different one. The total seems small, but since it is Scripture, it is true.

 ### The Martyred Saints

Revelation 7:9-17, *"After this I beheld, and, lo, a **great multitude, which no man could number**, of all nations, and kindreds, and people, and tongues, stood before the throne, and before the Lamb, clothed with white robes, and palms in their hands; And cried with a loud voice, saying, Salvation to our God which sitteth upon the throne, and unto the Lamb. And all the angels stood round about the throne, and about the elders and the four beasts, and fell before the throne on their faces, and worshipped God, Saying, Amen: Blessing, and glory and wisdom, and thanksgiving, and honor, and power, and might, be unto our God forever and ever. Amen. And one of the elders answered, saying unto me, What are these which are arrayed in white robes? and whence came they? And I said unto him, Sir, thou knowest. And he said to me, **These are they** which **came out of great***

67

tribulation, and have washed their robes, and made them white in the blood of the Lamb. Therefore are they before the throne of God, and serve him day and night in his temple: and he that sitteth on the throne shall dwell among them. They shall hunger no more, neither thirst any more; neither shall the sun light on them, nor any heat. For the Lamb which is in the midst of the throne shall feed them, and shall lead them unto living fountains of waters: and God shall wipe away all tears from their eyes."

After the 144,000 were sealed, the next event John saw in chapter 7, was a multitude of people *"which no man could number"* emerging from all the nations of earth. He viewed them worshipping God and dressed in white (those were not the 144,000). These have come out of **great tribulation** (v. 14). This multitude has obeyed unto death. They will not hunger, thirst, or be in exposure to sun or heat. These have been martyred; they were either killed with the sword or lost their homes and possessions to die from exposure. They entered heaven in sadness, but God will wipe away all their tears (v. 17); they will rejoice. Being obedient unto death, these are tribulation martyrs.

The "key" of doubled prophecy continues to apply. Please make a mental note of verse order; there is a consistent doubled order of events.

The 144,000 following the Lamb in Revelation 14:1-5 were paralleled in Revelation 7:4. Now, a **second** doubled prophecy regards the **martyrs**:

Revelation 15:2, *"And I saw as it were a sea of glass mingled with fire: and them that had **gotten the victory over the beast**, and over his image, and over his mark, and over the number of his name, stand on the sea of glass, having the*

68

harps of God."

This mention of them is brief. It is known from Scripture, the only possible victory over the beast is a spiritual one; those believers were martyred. That is the **second** vision's record of the ones dying for their faith. The above verses and Revelation 7:9-17 both record the tribulation martyrs. In both visions John saw the 144,000 overcomers and after them he saw the martyrs.

Revelation has given an account for two groups of believers, each have become acceptable to God through obedience. They chose different **courses** of obedience. That explains why Jesus told the Church of Thyatira, He would cast them into **great tribulation** (pressure) unless they repented (Revelation 2:22). Believers had the option to receive correction; those refusing to repent but keeping faith later became martyrs.

2 Corinthians 10:6 says that **after** Christian obedience is complete, God is ready to avenge all disobedience. In the fifth seal, judgment comes **after** the **martyrs** are killed (Revelation 6:11). According to those, wrath can be expected to begin upon the ungodly. The wrath judgments of God begin **after** all martyrs are gone and while the overcomers are cared for. God's wrath is **not** upon any of His people (1 Thessalonians 1:10, 5:9). Overcomers are sealed and still on earth waiting for Jesus' return. They will not receive the wrath judgments; that is proven by Revelation 9:4, the fifth wrath judgment. The locusts torment men that *"...have **not** the seal of God in their foreheads."* They are on earth, but protected.

The Seventh Seal

 Revelation 8:1-5, *"And when he had opened the seventh seal, there was silence in heaven about the space of half an hour. And I saw the seven angels which stood before God; and to them were given seven trumpets. And another angel*

69

came and stood at the altar, having a golden censer; and there was given unto him much incense, that he should offer it with the prayers of all the saints upon the golden altar which was before the throne. And the smoke of the incense which came with the prayers of the saints, ascended up before God out of the angel's hand. And the angel took the censer, and filled it with fire of the altar, and cast it into the earth: and there were voices, and thunderings, and lightnings, and an earthquake."

Where was John observing these proceedings from? Verse 3 says that he watched an angel offering incense at the altar while there was silence in heaven. In order to watch this angel, he must have been **inside** the temple of heaven.

 A parallel prophecy, the second vision with a different view is found in Revelation 15:5-8:

"And after that I looked, and, behold, the temple of the tabernacle of the testimony in heaven was opened: And the seven angels came out of the temple, having the seven plagues, clothed in pure and white linen, and having their breasts girded with golden girdles. And one of the four beasts gave unto the seven angels seven golden vials full of the wrath of God, who liveth forever and ever. And the temple was filled with smoke from the glory of God, and from his power; and no man was able to enter into the temple, till the seven plagues of the seven angels were fulfilled."

Where was John as he described this passage? In verse 5, the temple of the tabernacle was opened; in verse 6, the angels came out. John was in heaven, but he was **outside** the temple. The temple

70

was filled with smoke from the glory of God and the offering of much incense (Revelation 8:3). No man was able to enter the temple; so naturally with no one able to worship, the result would have been the "silence" of the first vision in Revelation 8:1.

Those prophetic visions are giving the same **message**, but the descriptions are different—like the kine and corn from Genesis.

GOD'S WRATH

The wrath judgments of God are poured out upon earth. **None of the saints of God are recipients of His wrath**. They are either cared for in a place of provision or with Him through martyrdom. John viewed the sealed 144,000, and then he saw the **martyrs in heaven; those comprise the church. God deals with His** church; then in chapter 8, the seventh seal is opened initiating seven wrath judgments on the wicked.

The Bible says seven plagues of wrath take place. Each of the seven plagues is addressed in two passages of Scripture. These wrath judgments are described by the seven trumpet and vial judgments. The trumpet and vial judgments are the same as the "kine and corn"; they are doubled prophecy telling the exact same story. Both sets of Scriptures follow the same chronology; they also have a common subject. Unlike the previous seven seals, the seven judgments take place in order.

The wrath judgments are administered by angels. They begin **after** the **second** beast has risen. That is proven by Revelation 16:2, *"And the first went, and poured his vial upon the earth; and there fell a noisome and grievous sore upon the men which had the mark of the beast, and upon them which worshipped his image."* The first wrath judgment begins **after** the second beast (Antichrist) has risen because the *mark* and *image* are founded by it (Revelation 13:15, 16).

The Seven Trumpet and Vial Judgments

1	Revelation 8:7	**EARTH**	Revelation 16:2

*"The first angel sounded, and there followed hail and fire mingled with blood, and they were cast upon the **earth**: and the third part of the trees was burnt up, and all the green grass was burnt up."*

*"And the first went, and poured out his vial upon the **earth**; and there fell a noisome and grievous sore upon the men which had the mark of the beast, and upon them which worshipped his image."*

2	Revelation 8:8, 9	**SEA**	Revelation 16:3

*"And the second angel sounded, and as it were a great mountain burning with fire was cast into the **sea**: and the third part of the sea became **blood**; And the third part of the creatures which were in the **sea**, and had life, **died**; and the third part of the ships were destroyed."*

*"And the second angel poured out his vial upon the **sea**; and it became as the **blood** of a dead man: and every living soul **died** in the **sea**."*

*"And the third angel sounded, and there fell a great star from heaven, burning as it were a lamp, and it fell upon the third part of the **rivers**, and upon the **fountains of waters**; And the name of the star is called Wormwood: and the third part of the waters became wormwood; and many men died of the waters, because they were bitter."*

*"And the third angel poured out his vial upon the **rivers** and **fountains of waters**; and they became blood. And I heard the angel of the waters say, Thou art righteous, oh Lord, which art, and wast, and shalt be, because thou hast judged thus. For they have shed the blood of saints and prophets, and thou hast given them blood to drink; for they are worthy."*

*"And the fourth angel sounded, and the third part of the **sun** was smitten, and the third part of the moon, and the third part of the stars; so as the third part of them was darkened, and the day shone not for a third part of it, and the night likewise."*

*"And the fourth angel poured out his vial upon the **sun**; and power was given unto him to scorch men with fire. And men were scorched with great heat, and blasphemed the name of God, which hath power over these plagues: and they repented not to give him glory."*

"And the fifth angel sounded, and I saw a star fall from heaven unto the earth: and to him was given the key of the bottomless pit. And he opened the bottomless pit; and there arose a smoke out of the pit, as the smoke of a great furnace; and the sun and the air were **darkened** *by reason of the smoke of the pit."*

"And the fifth angel poured out his vial upon the seat of the beast; and his kingdom was full of **darkness** *and they gnawed their tongues for pain, And blasphemed the God of heaven because of their pains and their sores, and repented not of their deeds."*

"And the sixth angel sounded, and I heard a voice from the four horns of the golden altar which is before God, Saying to the sixth angel which had the trumpet, Loose the four angels which are bound in the **great river Euphrates.** *And the four angels were loosed, which were prepared for an hour, and a day, and a month, and a year, for to slay the third part of men. And the number of the army of the horsemen were two hundred thousand thousand: and I heard the number of them."*

"And the sixth angel poured out his vial upon the **great river Euphrates;** *and the water thereof was dried up, that the way of the kings of the east might be prepared."*

GREAT VOICES, LIGHTNINGS, THUNDERING, EARTHQUAKE, HAIL, VOICES

Revelation 11:15, 19	Revelation 16:17, 18, 21

*"And the seventh angel sounded; and there were **great voices** in heaven, saying, The kingdoms of this world are become the kingdoms of our Lord, and of his Christ; and he shall reign for ever and ever. [19]And the temple of God was opened in heaven, and there was seen in his temple the ark of his testament: and there were **lightnings**, and **voices**, and **thunderings**, and an **earthquake**, and **great hail**."*

*"And the seventh angel poured out his vial into the air; and there came a **great voice** out of the temple of heaven, from the throne, saying, It is done. And there were **voices**, and **thunders**, and **lightnings**; and there was a great **earthquake**, such as was not since men were upon the earth, so mighty an earthquake, and so great. [21]And there fell upon men a **great hail** out of heaven, every stone about the weight of a talent: and men blasphemed God because of the plague of the hail; for the plague thereof was exceeding great."*

An identical series of events has occurred in two separate visions. The seventh judgment (directly above) is the **final** wrath judgment on the wicked. The seventh judgment **also** encompasses the **return** of Jesus, so the seventh wrath **judgment** also **contains** events included in the sixth **seal**. The sixth seal is the wrath of the **Lamb, the return of Christ**; He overcomes all the wicked and establishes the millennial reign.

The two descriptions of the above seventh judgment **verify** the **end**: *"The kingdoms of this world **are become** the **kingdoms of our Lord**, and of his Christ; and **he shall reign** forever and ever"* (the trumpets), and *"It is done"* (the vials). The millennial reign begins after the kingdoms of earth are made subject to Christ.

In the seventh wrath judgment, the **first** phenomenon is the sound of a **great** voice or **great** voices. Those descriptions both equal a **shout**. 1 Thessalonians 4:16 says, *"For the Lord himself shall descend from heaven with a **shout**..."* A **shout** and a **great voice** is interchangeable. Either way, the **message** is the same: a **loud** voice. These Revelation pieces fit perfectly with other Scripture and will be addressed in the next chapter.

CHANGED

The timing for the greatest of mysteries is given in Revelation—the "rapture" and the "return of Jesus." These next passages should resolve the schedule for that event (one event, several features). Look at the *rapture* (being changed) and return of Jesus according to Scripture. That multiple occurrence event is recorded in both visions of the trumpet and vial judgments.

"Behold, I show you a mystery; We shall not all sleep, but we shall all be changed, In a moment, in the twinkling of an eye, at the last trump: for the trumpet shall sound, and the dead shall be raised incorruptible, and we shall be changed" (1 Corinthians 15:51, 52). The *mystery* in that verse is the rapture; it occurs at the last trump. In Revelation, seven trumpets are blown in the wrath judgments. According to 1 Corinthians, the rapture will occur at the seventh trump, the **last** one.

Buried within the first vision's trumpet judgments, Revelation 10:7 says: *"But in the days of the voice of the **seventh** [last] angel, when he shall **begin** to sound, the **mystery** of God should be **finished**...."* The mystery (being changed) is at the beginning of the last angel's trumpet; there is the **rapture**. The mystery is very clear and easy to understand when the 1 Corinthians reference is included. Revelation 10:7 is located **after the conclusion** of the **sixth** trumpet judgment.

The second vision's vial judgments contain the **same timing** for this event—**after the conclusion** of the **sixth** vial judgment. The event is worded somewhat differently because it speaks of Jesus' return, instead of the mystery of being changed. Upcoming **Scripture** proves Jesus' **return** and the **rapture** occur **simultaneously**.

I Thessalonians 5:2 says, *"For yourselves know perfectly*

*that the **day of the Lord** so cometh as a **thief** in the night."* The *"day of the Lord"* (Jesus' return) comes as a thief.

Within the second vision's vial judgments, **after** the sixth vial is completed and **before** the seventh vial, Revelation says, *"Behold, I come as a **thief**..."* (Revelation 16:15). That is reference to the **return of Christ**, i.e., *"the day of the Lord."* It is very clear and easy to understand when including 1 Thessalonians.

Jesus' return/rapture is recorded in the vial and trumpet judgments; it is at the same chronological **location** within the doubled-vision. Neither context of those two passages continues the thought of verses surrounding them. They are **not significant** to the text, which begs the question: what are they doing there? God put them right where they are to **teach His servants**. People not having His Holy Spirit will never perceive those hidden truths. When considering their **location chronologically** to the seventh and last **judgment** (trumpet or vial), they have **great significance!** Jesus revealed the rapture and when He will return! He **disclosed** the **timing** for the mystery of the ages.

Scripture substantiates that the rapture and return of Jesus are **positively** different phases of the **same event**; they happen simultaneously.

*"For this we say unto you by the word of the Lord, that we which are **alive and remain unto the coming of the Lord** shall not prevent them which are asleep. For the **Lord himself shall descend from heaven** with a **shout**, with the voice of the archangel, and with the **trump** of God: and the dead in Christ shall rise first, **Then we which are alive and remain shall be caught up together with them in the clouds, to meet the Lord in the air**: and so shall we ever be with the Lord"* (1 Thessalonians 4:15-17).

79

At the end of the previous chapter, the **seventh** (last) trumpet and vial **judgment** were addressed. A **great** voice or **great** voices **begin** the seventh judgment; it is the **first** phenomenon for both. In 1 Thessalonians 4:16, the **first** phenomenon is *"a shout"* **as** the Lord **descends**. The **great** *voice* or *voices* are equivalent to a *"shout."* They are all synonymous; they are **loud**. The seventh trumpet, the seventh vial, and 1 Thessalonians 4:16 **all** agree and **begin** the Lord's return **loudly**.

Jesus' **return**, the **resurrection** of the dead, and the **rapture all** happen at the **same time** (1 Thessalonians 4:15-17). The resurrection and rapture are **also united** in 1 Corinthians 15:51 and 52. Those are **all** in agreement.

In the sixth **seal**, *"...the great day of his wrath is come..."* (Revelation 6:12-17). In the seventh trumpet, *"...The kingdoms of this world **are become** the kingdoms of our Lord, and of his Christ; and he shall reign for ever and ever"* (Revelation 11:15). In the seventh vial, *"...It is done"* (Revelation 16:17). Jesus is shown to tread the "winepress of wrath" and is declared *"...KING OF KINGS, AND LORD OF LORDS"* (Revelation 19:11-16); those Scriptures **entwine** with one another.

A basic overview indicates those events are interwoven. During the seventh seal, seven wrath judgments are dispensed by angels. At the beginning of the seventh angel's judgment, there is a shout. The sixth seal is opened; the wicked on earth see the Lord coming in the air. He is coming to tread the **winepress** of God's wrath (dispensed by Jesus); the resurrection and rapture occur. Believers meet Jesus in the air during His return. He destroys the wicked and the government of Antichrist (2 Thessalonians 2:8). Then Jesus begins the millennial reign; His servants are with Him via resurrection and rapture.

Jesus does not return two different times nor are there two separate raptures. There is only **one** glorious return of Christ and

one rapture. That singular return is expressed in the contents of the following Scriptures:

- 1 Thessalonians 4:14-17
- 1 Corinthians 15:50-54
- Matthew 24:29-31

The description agrees with **all Scriptures, including the Gospels** (upcoming study).

The event called the *rapture* encompasses those sealed, provided for and protected by God during periods of tribulation and wrath. Revelation 2:17 and 3:4 indicate they were eating hidden manna and clothed in white. The name of God was written on them (Revelation 3:12). Only the "sealed overcomers" remain on earth awaiting rapture; they are the only believers still alive. **All** others have been **martyred** in battle or exposure while resisting the first beast, or by execution for refusing the mark of the second beast. The martyrs are waiting for glorified bodies and are already with the Lord in spirit. They receive resurrected bodies at His return.

The sealed are protected and provided for throughout eras of tribulation and wrath. When the Lord returns, Ephesians 5:27 is fulfilled through resurrection and rapture. *"That he might present it to himself a glorious church, **not having spot**, or **wrinkle**, or any such thing; but that it should be **holy** and **without blemish**."*

The Gospel passages indicating an early rapture possibility, *"the one will be taken, and the other left,"* and *"when these things **begin** to come to pass, then look up, and lift up your heads; for your **redemption** draweth nigh"* will be addressed in the next chapter. They fit flawlessly into the above presented interpretation.

* * * * *

John's first and second visions start with differing perspectives. John is in "space" to see the first vision's 144,000 get

81

sealed (Revelation 7:1-4). He is on earth (Mt. Zion) during the second vision (Revelation 14:1). These dual visions reveal events included in, and subsequent to, the third seal. Provision begins during the third seal. Those believers are hidden until the rapture.

 Reviewing **parallel** events recorded by the dual prophetic vision reveals the following chronology:

FIRST VISION	SECOND VISION
Revelation 7:4-8 The 144,000	Revelation 14:1-5 The 144,000
Revelation 7:9-17 The martyred	Revelation 14:12, 15:2-4 The martyred
Revelation 8:1 Silence in heaven	Revelation 15:8 No man able to enter temple
Revelation 8:1-5 John **inside** the tabernacle in heaven	Revelation 15:5-8 John **outside** the tabernacle in heaven
Revelation 8:4 Smoke	Revelation 15:8 Smoke
Revelation 8:7 Earth	Revelation 16:2 Earth
Revelation 8:8, 9 Sea	Revelation 16:3 Sea
Revelation 8:10, 11 Rivers	Revelation 16:4-6 Rivers
Revelation 8:12 Sun	Revelation 16:8, 9 Sun
Revelation 9:1, 2 Darkened	Revelation 16:10, 11 Darkness
Revelation 9:13-16 River Euphrates	Revelation 16:12 River Euphrates
Revelation 10:7 The Rapture, 1 Corinthians 15:51, 52	Revelation 16:15 Return of Jesus, 1 Thessalonians 5:2
Revelation 11:15, 19 **Great** voice in heaven, lightning, thunderings, earthquake, hail and voice	Revelation 16:17, 18, 21 **Great** voices, lightning, thunderings, earthquake, hail and voice

Thirteen events or subjects have been listed in chronological order. These thirteen events are identical in general message although two separate visions. Even the greatest doubter should need to admit this chronology could not be coincidence. The prophetic meaning is identical to the kine and corn of Pharaoh's dream; Joseph said the message was "*one*." By biblical precedent, the doubled prophetic communication means: "*...the thing is* **established** *by God, and* **God will shortly bring it to pass**" (Genesis 41:32).

These events are coming **soon**!

A UNIQUE VIEWPOINT

Previously, there has been a lot of controversy concerning the pre-tribulation or post-tribulation rapture. Scriptures exist that can be used to support either. The Bible does **not** bring confusion or conflict. A proper viewpoint is needed to perceive the inter-relationship for all of God's Word. A closer examination will differentiate between Scriptures; viewing overcomers who are provided for, helps bring clarity for the affiliation of Scriptures.

> *"And there appeared a great wonder in heaven; a woman clothed with the sun, and the moon under her feet, and upon her head a crown of twelve stars: And she being with child cried, travailing in birth, and pained to be delivered. And there appeared another wonder in heaven; and behold a great red dragon, having seven heads and ten horns, and seven crowns upon his heads. And his tail drew the third part of the stars of heaven, and it cast them to the earth: and the dragon stood before the woman which was ready to be delivered, for to devour her child as soon as it was born. And she brought forth a man child, who was to rule all nations with a rod of iron: and her child was caught up unto God, and to his throne. And the woman fled into the wilderness, where she hath a place prepared of God, that they should feed her there a thousand two hundred and three score days"* (Revelation 12:1-6).

Obviously, the *woman* represents God's people from the time of the twelve patriarchs (twelve stars). Jesus came out of that *woman* as her child. The children of Abraham are the people of God (the woman) of whom Christ was born. Then the **child** of Abraham (Jesus) returned to God and His throne to be the resurrected King of kings. The woman flees from the devil (dragon) and **is divinely cared** for 1,260 days (3½ years). The passage reveals war in heaven between God's angels and the devil. Satan loses and is cast to the earth. Then in Revelation 12:11, there are those that *"...loved not their lives unto the death."* (Please open to chapter 12.)

✠ Looking for doubled-vision characteristics (as with the trumpets and vials) reveals chapter 12 contains such a doubled-vision.

1) The **Dragon** is common in both visions and is the enemy of the woman (vv. 4, 13).

2) The woman takes refuge in the **wilderness** where she is provided for three and one half years (vv. 6, 14).

3) The Dragon **persecutes** those **not** under God's divine provision (the spiritually immature "seed" of the woman) (vv. 11, 17).

Two time frames are within the dual vision:

1) Before the devil is cast out of heaven

2) After the devil is cast out of heaven

Possibly, the total time of provision for the woman (God's spiritually mature people) will be seven years (2 x 3½).

In verse 17, the dragon went to make war with the woman's "seed." A *seed* is not a mature plant. The woman (spiritually **mature** believers) is protected (hidden) from the face of the serpent. However, the seed (spiritually **immature,** offspring) is not protected. Verse 11 states, *"...they loved not their lives unto the death."* Those are martyrs.

There are **two** different groups of **believers**. The parable of the ten virgins distinguishes two groups of believers. The apostle Paul spoke of both spiritual and carnal Christians.

*"And to the woman were given two wings of a great **eagle**, that she might fly into the **wilderness**, into her place, where she is nourished for a time, and times, and half a time, from the face of the*

85

serpent" (Revelation 12:14). Notice the bolded words identifying the means of escape for the woman and where she goes. She is hidden.

A word from the above verse reveals both metaphorical and spiritual understanding. **Look** at the **same principle**, via a **biblically established** metaphor. Exodus 19:4 says, *"Ye have seen what I did unto the Egyptians, and how I bear you on **eagles' wings**, and **brought you unto myself**."* God was describing His miraculous delivery and **provision** for Israel. He delivered and protected them from Pharaoh to bring them to Himself. (They didn't leave earth.) God describes His **provision** as bearing them on **eagles'** wings. The woman of Revelation 12 is described as having the **wings of an eagle** for escape. A wonderful principle is divulged which all believers need to grasp.

Jesus spoke about this principle and **eagles** in the Gospels. In the New Testament, **eagles** are **only found** in passages declaring **aspects** of the **end-time**!

> *"I tell you, in that night there shall be two men in one bed; the one shall be taken, and the other shall be left. Two women shall be grinding together; the one shall be taken, and the other left. Two men shall be in a field; the one shall be taken, and the other left. And they answered and said unto him, **Where, Lord**? And he said unto them, Wheresoever the body is, thither will the **eagles** be gathered together"* (Luke 17:34-37).

Some have believed this passage details the rapture. Within these verses, two people appear to be doing the same things. They **appear** to be alike. In the literal Greek language, the phrase *"shall be taken"* means to "receive near," i.e., "associate with." The phrase, *"the other left"* means, "to send forth." One of the groups

Jesus distinguished is "drawn near/associate with," while the other is "sent forth."

His disciples perceived those "drawing near," are going somewhere so they asked Him, *"Where, Lord"* (v. 37)? This passage **concludes** with *"Where, Lord"* and **then** the **answer**: *"...Wheresoever the body is, thither will the **eagles** be gathered together."* Jesus referred to the ones going somewhere as "eagles." The passage teaches that **eagles** are going to **gather together somewhere**. The eagles are the group that is "taken."

God **divinely provides** for the eagles as He previously demonstrated in Exodus. Eagles represent God's people going to His **earthly** provision.

In Revelation, **eagles** are the means for God's people to receive refuge. In the Gospels, Jesus uses **eagles** to describe those who are to be "taken." In Exodus, **eagles** describe God's deliverance, provision, and bringing His people to Himself while on earth.

To bring clarity to the concept of eagles representing provision, I will share a true story. Claire, my son Joshua's wife, was looking out a window in their country home. Some large animal entrails were piled along the edge of a wooded area. A flock of ravens was very happy to find the carcass entrails; the ground was covered with snow, making food scarce. As she watched them gather at the pile day by day, she realized the implication of Luke 17:37, *"...Wheresoever the body is, thither will the eagles be gathered together."* Jesus used the same illustration that Claire observed with the ravens. The eagles will gather to "the body," as the ravens did to the entrails. Both are for **provision**—like the provision for the woman in Revelation 12:6, 14. The **entire** text of Luke 17:30-37 is preparatory to that gathering.

Eagles' wings are the woman's means for escape from the dragon. Overcomers escape the devil and also God's judgments of wrath. His provision is beyond the physical and natural norms for this world, the same as He demonstrated with Pharaoh.

Some people interpret Luke's passage to mean the rapture. Scriptures explaining the rapture display believers being *"caught up"* **to** Jesus during His return to meet Him **in the air** (1 Thessalonians 4:15-17). The context of Luke indicates it is for **provision** because of the eagles' metaphor. That assessment is confirmed by another Scripture.

Matthew 24:28 reads, *"For wheresoever the **carcass** is, there will the **eagles** be gathered together."* The use of the word *carcass* (in Greek) brings clear understanding to what Jesus meant; eagles gather at a carcass. A *carcass* is a "body"—a **dead** one, i.e., **provision** for an eagle. At the rapture, there is no reason for the church to meet the Lord at a **dead** body because believers have glorified bodies, no longer needing physical sustenance. By context, the passage teaches provision for overcomers. Recall the ravens.

The eagle' contexts from Luke and Matthew bear information concerning **two differing time periods**. Those descriptions contribute **instruction and warning** for *taken* believers.

In Luke, a group of **accepted** people are going somewhere. They are **not to delay, take provisions, or return back**. Immediate obedience is required when commanded to "go." The disciples asked Jesus **where** they were going; He responded: *"...**Wheresoever** the **body** is, there will the eagles be gathered together."* Luke's passage is instruction for **traveling** to **go** to the place of provision. It is instruction for "eagles" that are **in route to** the "body." They must go without delay, provisions or returning.

In Matthew's Gospel, instruction is for **after** eagles **arrive** and **are receiving provision**.

*"Wherefore if they shall say unto you, Behold, he is in the desert; **go not forth**: behold, he is in the secret chambers; **believe it not**. For as the lightning cometh out of the east, and shineth even unto the west; so shall also the coming of the Son of man be. For wheresoever the carcass is, **there will the eagles be gathered together"** (Matthew 24:26-28).*

Jesus is warning those **previously gathered** at the carcass; He said *"go not forth."* They are to **stay** and not be deceived if they **hear** He is in the desert or secret chambers; He said *"believe it not."* They must stay at the carcass **until** He **appears** as lightning shining across the sky. **He will rapture them from where the carcass is.** Believers need to know that. If they understand, they will not leave and be deceived by false Christs and prophets performing signs and miracles (Matthew 24:24). Matthew's instructions are *"believe it not"* and *"go not forth."* The directives in Luke and Matthew each apply to a **different season.**

A description of Jesus' return is given in Matthew 24:29-31. He comes in the clouds of heaven with power and glory. He gathers His elect from one end of heaven to the other. That description is verified in Mark 13:26, 27. His people are raptured **during** His return and **with** the sound of a **trumpet**; 1 Thessalonians 4:15, 16 depict an identical portrayal. That scenario is the only one capable of accommodating the Gospels, Epistles and Revelation so that **none** of the Scriptures are in **conflict.**

At this point, the **difference** between Jesus' "glorious return/rapture," and when *"the Son of man is **revealed"*** (Luke 17:30) needs to be clarified. Jesus' return and the rapture have been confused with Jesus' revealing (literally in Greek: "take off the cover"). The **revealing** of Jesus is a part of "provision passages" concerning eagles. Luke 17:30, 31 say,

*"Even thus shall it be in the day when the **Son of man is revealed**. In that day, he which shall be upon the housetop, and his stuff in the house, **let him not come down to take it away**: and he that is in the field, **let him likewise not return back**."*

The Scripture teaches about when Jesus is revealed and then gives instruction concerning related actions. It does not describe what is associated with the rapture and return of Christ.

Look again at the rapture in 1 Corinthians 15:51, 52: *"...but we shall all be **changed, In a moment, in the twinkling of an eye**, at the last trump...."* Also 1 Thessalonians 4:17, *"Then we which are alive and remain shall be **caught up** together with them in the clouds to **meet the Lord in the air**: and so shall we ever be with the Lord."* If the "revealing" would be at the time of rapture, there would be no reason to instruct believers **not** to go back and get their *"stuff in the house"* or *"return"* to the field. They would be raptured, i.e., **"changed in the twinkling of an eye,"** and **"meet the Lord in the air."** They would no longer be on earth in mortal bodies to return for earthly things! By context, the **revealing** from Luke 17 is **not** the rapture!

The passage pertains to believers who **wait** at the carcass for Christ's return. Jesus provides for and protects them **on earth**. He has only **revealed** Himself to the 144,000 of Revelation 14:1. They are the only ones with the Lamb. In the parable of ten virgins, only five went in to be with the Lord.

Please consider: Jesus reveals Himself to His people in their **present** lives. That is how every believer started on the path of salvation. By **spirit**, Jesus meets their needs. He reveals Himself as He saves them and abides with them. In the future, He **will reveal** Himself again in a **very special** way. His "taken" people will experience His manifest presence—a powerful **spiritual presence**

90

according to the wording of Revelation 14:1. He is metaphorically referred to as a **Lamb**, indicating His presence is **not** physical. By spirit, He is in the midst of believers while providing for them.

"*And I looked, and, lo, a **Lamb** stood on Mt. Zion, and **with him** a hundred forty and four thousand, having his Father's name written in their foreheads*" (Revelation 14:1). This Scripture pictures how some are "drawn near" to Christ. The revealing is **not** the return of Christ. **Only** the 144,000 are aware of His presence; others do **not** know He is there. That narrative does not fit His return; there is no **lightning flashing across the sky for all to see** (Matthew 24:27). It doesn't describe believers, "*...caught up together with them in the clouds to meet the Lord in the air...*" (1 Thessalonians 4:17).

For provision, **only** the "*firstfruits*" of Revelation 14:4 have received the "*...Father's name **written** in their foreheads*" (Revelation 14:1). At the conclusion of Revelation, all of God's servants have His name written in their foreheads (Revelation 22:3, 4).

Following, is another passage some will use to support the pre-tribulation rapture.

"*And then shall they see the Son of man coming in a cloud with power and great glory. And when these things **begin** to come to pass, then look up, and lift up your heads; for your **redemption** draweth nigh. And he spake to them a parable; Behold the fig tree, and all the trees; When they now shoot forth, ye see and know of your own selves that summer is now nigh at hand. So likewise ye, when ye see these things come to pass, know ye that the kingdom of God is nigh at hand*" (Luke 21:27-31).

Many Christians judge that *redemption* means "rapture."

They believe the rapture happens at the beginning of end-time events: "…*when these things **begin** to come to pass.*"

The passage is actually **part** of a **larger** account for the end-time. It does not stand alone so as to explain the timing of the rapture. Instead, it fits together with other Scriptures depicting more details of the **differing aspects** of the end-time.

If applied to the rapture directly as it reads, it would clash with the organization of all previously studied Scriptures. It would also **conflict** with Mark 13:26, 27, which say,

> "*And **then** shall they see the Son of man **coming in the clouds** with great power and glory. And **then** shall he send his angels, and **shall gather his elect** from the four winds, from the uttermost of the earth to the uttermost part of heaven.*"

Jesus returns and gathers His people at the **end** of **tribulation** (Mark 13:24)—not at the beginning, as it could be understood from Luke. The understanding of those Gospels would contradict one with another. If Scriptures seem to contradict, they have not been properly understood.

There are ideal applications for these "pre-tribulation passages" to fit the end-time picture. As incidents **begin** to occur, look for **redemption** (Luke 21:28), which corresponds perfectly with Revelation 14:1-5 (**redeemed** 144,000 with Jesus); it also joins with the timing of Revelation 7:2, 3 (the sealing of God's servants before the earth is hurt). Redemption shares the **same schedule** as provision passages; they are both at the **beginning** of the tribulation events.

Redemption is fulfilled by the sealed 144,000: "*…These were **redeemed** from among men, being the **firstfruits** unto God and to the Lamb*" (Revelation 14:4). The *redeemed* are the ones who will, "*look up and lift up your heads; for your* **redemption** *draweth nigh.*" They are **sealed, redeemed** early and protected from famine, the first beast, second beast, and the wrath of God. *Redemption* is administered to the 144,000 *redeemed.* They are on earth through it all, but protected. The "fifth wrath judgment" bears **proof**:

> "*And there came out of the smoke locusts upon the earth: and unto them was given power, as the scorpions of the earth have power. And it was commanded them that they should not hurt the grass of the earth, neither any green thing, neither any tree; but* **only** *those men which have* **not** *the* **seal of God in their foreheads**" (Revelation 9:3, 4).

The sealing of God's people occurs before the earth is "hurt"; hurting the earth causes famine (Revelation 6:6; 7:3, 4). That occurs at the **beginning** of the end-time events (the famine of Matthew 24:7). The fifth wrath judgment is administered while the second beast/Antichrist rules the earth. That is toward the **end** of the tribulation. The redeemed are the sealed; they are where the carcass is and escape the wrath judgments while Antichrist is in power.

Additional gospel passages also need to be addressed in order to cover all passages churches use to support a pre-tribulation rapture. These two passages are linked together so as to establish the timing for Christ's return, but there are differing conditions on earth concerning each passage. These passages should **not** be combined as though portraying the same event.

> "*And then shall appear the sign of the Son of man in heaven: and then shall all the tribes of the earth mourn, and they shall see the Son of man* **coming** *in the clouds of heaven with power and with great glory*" (Matthew 24:30).
> "*But as the days of Noe were, so shall also the* **coming** *of the*

Son of man be" (Matthew 24:37).

Matthew 24:30 and 37, detail a *"coming"* of the Lord. Many think the coming (*parousia; Strong's* #3952) in verse 37 confirms the timing for the return of Jesus in verse 30. That association needs to be explored.

Verse 30 certainly describes Jesus' return; *parousia*, translated *coming* is utilized. *Parousia* signifies "**being near.**" That is the **first** defined use when taken literally from its root words. According to the **textual setting**, its English translation can be **either** *coming* **or** *presence*.

There are two differing **contexts** concerning these passages. **Prior** to Christ's **return** in verse 30, conditions on earth are described in verse 21: *"For then shall be **great tribulation**, such as was **not since the beginning** of the **world** to this time, no, nor ever shall be."* In verse 24, **false** Christs and prophets are showing great signs and wonders. In verse 22, conditions on earth are becoming sparse, no one would survive and the time is shortened so the elect can stay alive. That is how the world looks prior to Christ's return in verse 30.

In verses 37 and 38 there are **different** descriptions for human circumstances; society is again depicted and Jesus' *parousia* is declared. This time Jesus likened prior social environments to the days of Noah: *"...eating and drinking, marrying and giving in marriage, **until** the day that Noe entered into the ark"* (v. 38). Jesus said life continued as usual for all people **until** Noah entered the ark.

"Life as usual," leads to *parousia* in a different sense than the *parousia* of Jesus' return. Conditions before **taking** His people to a place of provision are **life as usual**. Prior to His return, He spoke of ***great tribulation***. The conditions in society are very different although both passages utilize the same Greek word which

94

can express **either** *coming* **or** *presence*.

Once Jesus explained conditions prior to His return (v. 30), there was no reason for **repetition**; Jesus was **not reiterating** what He taught in **prior** verses. He was revealing a different phase of the end-time. Verses 36-44 are about His *being near* as a different subject, and the context verses reveal a different usage for the word He incorporated.

In the days of Noah, God interceded to provide Noah and his family an escape from judgment. They were on earth but spared the judgment of the flood. Jesus used that illustration to present *parousia* in verse 37. The same escape from judgment applies during the end-time occurrences. The *parousia* concerning *the days of Noah* is for **provision**.

Social happenings preceding provision continue; verse 40 says, *"Then shall two be in the field; the one shall be taken, and the other left."* That same statement was previously studied in Luke 17:36. It is the **context** for when Jesus' said, *"...Wheresoever the* **body is**, *thither will the* **eagles** *be* **gathered** *together"* (Luke 17:37). The *"...one shall being taken, and the other left"* involves **eagles** gathering for provision in Luke's gospel. In Matthew *one taken and the other left* is associated with *parousia* as the days of Noah (the timing for provision); *one taken and the other left* is recorded by both gospels and both indicate the time of provision. That is not coincidental.

There are ten different words that were translated into English as "taken" in the New Testament. One of them *apairo* #522, means "to lift off or remove;" it would be an appropriate word to use if the rapture (being caught up) was expressed within passages stating *"one will be **taken** and the other left,"* but it wasn't used. Instead both gospels use *paralambano* (#3880), meaning "to receive **near**." The distinction between those two words expressing *taken,* presents an available ability to accurately communicate the

95

rapture, but the appropriate word to do it **was not used**. In those passages, "rapture" was not the topic. Linguistics supports the **provision** point of view.

The Gospels (Matthew 24:16-28, 37-44 and Mark 13:15-23) expound on two being in the field, one taken and the other left; two grinding at the mill, one taken, the other left; he that is on the house top not go down to take anything out; he that is in the field not to return for a garment; and it will be as the days of Noah. Those references are referring to the time of **provision** for overcoming Christians.

Look closely at Mark 13:15-20: it is easy to see God's elect are still on earth. The elect are not raptured to **escape** earth's afflictions; instead, the days of affliction are **shortened** for the **survival** of God's elect.

The time of provision **coincides** with "the abomination of desolation" happening in Israel; those in Judea must flee to the mountains (Matthew 24:15; Mark 13:14, probably Messianic Jews). Those verses exclusively address people in Israel; the timing to flee to the mountains corresponds with the balance of the earth's elect traveling to the carcass.

Revelation identifies the sealing of overcomers while life is still carried on "as usual"—**before** the third seal's world famine; then earthly conditions begin deteriorating. In Matthew, life is as usual prior to Jesus' *parousia* for provision; those coincide.

"Life as usual" leading into provision, illuminates passages to bear significantly more meaning. If believers are not watching closely, "life as usual" could take them by surprise.

> *"And take **heed to yourselves**, lest at any time your hearts be over-charged with surfeiting, and drunkenness, and cares of this life, and **so that day come upon you unawares**. For **as a snare** shall it come upon all them that dwell on the*

*face of the whole earth. **Watch** ye therefore, and **pray always**, that ye **may be accounted worthy to escape** all these things that shall come to pass, and to stand before the Son of man"* (Luke 21:34-36).

In the Gospels, tribulation, false miracle-working prophets and poor conditions on earth exist before Jesus' **return**. Revelation also shows great tribulation, a false miracle-working prophet and six wrath judgments adversely affecting life on earth. Jesus' return **follows** those. The time of His return does **not arrive subtly** so as to catch anyone except **unbelievers** unaware. Believers know Jesus is returning soon; they are where eagles gather and were warned "not to be deceived" if they hear He is in the "desert" or "secret chambers" (Matthew 24:26). The above passage becomes very significant when comprehending the coming provision for believers.

The following compilation of Scriptures and a brief synopsis of each, aids in identifying the existence of believers being set apart and provided for on earth. Here are distinctive Scriptures supporting that group:

Revelation 7:3—servants of God sealed before earth is hurt
Revelation 6:6—oil and wine not hurt by black horseman
Isaiah 27:1-3—the Lord keeps a vineyard of wine from hurt
Revelation 12:6—woman fed in wilderness by God
Revelation 12:14—woman fed and protected from the devil
Luke 17:37—where the body is, the eagles gather
Matthew 24:28—where the carcass is, the eagles gather
Isaiah 65:8—found in a cluster; God doesn't destroy all
Zephaniah 2:3—you may be hidden in the day of anger
Luke 21:36—pray to be counted worthy to escape
Isaiah 26:20, 21—God's people hide as His fury passes

97

Revelation 2:17—overcomers eat of hidden manna
Isaiah 65:13-14—God's servants eat, drink; others hunger
Revelation 14:4—144,000 are God's redeemed firstfruits
Revelation 9:4—sealed, protected from wrath on earth
Matthew 25:1-13—some believers with Jesus; some not

The events yet to happen from the above-listed Scriptures **must be fulfilled**. There will be an era for a select group of believers to be cared for by God. That is a major difference between the end-time interpretation presented in this book and what others have taught throughout prior years.

Perceiving the Scriptures in the above manner goes "full circle" without contradiction or conflict by any Scripture. The assessment of this writing brings **harmony** and **clarity** to **all** passages concerning the end-time. There is no more debate as to whether pre-tribulation or post-tribulation rapture Scriptures are to be observed. The Scriptures are **all accurate** when viewed properly.

The concept of a group of believers being provided for on earth brings the uniformity. Prophetic verses are fulfilled; there are **no** conflicts for pre-tribulation vs. post-tribulation rapture Scriptures (chronology is accurately applied to both **provision** and Jesus' **return/rapture**); there is appropriate Greek word usage; passages of Scripture come alive with deeper meaning; the **Bible** interprets the Bible without necessity for human reasoning because all portions of the end-time make sense.

* * * * *

More is to be obtained in the end-time passage from Luke 17: *"Whosoever shall seek to save his life shall lose it; and whosoever shall lose his life shall preserve it"* (v. 33). Jesus was clarifying the **distinction** between two groups of people: those

98

being **taken** and those **left**. He was referencing His revealing (v. 30).

God implements a winnowing fork to separate two groups of believers. The person seeking to save his life must lose it (in a spiritual sense). Overcomers **voluntarily** lose ownership of their lives and **yield** themselves **completely** to God; they make Jesus the **Lord** and **Master** of their lives, obeying their Lord's Word (the Bible) and voice (His Spirit)—just as slaves obey a master. That is the kingdom of God activated **in** believers. Jesus said, *"...the kingdom of God is **within** you"* (Luke 17:21). God reigns from **within** believers (to be explained in "The Kingdom of God" chapter). In Revelation, those believers *"...follow the Lamb **whithersoever** he goeth..."* (Revelation 14:4). They do not follow the Lamb for a short distance or to a destination that **they** are comfortable with or that pleases **them**.

Such is the case with many believers who cling to a "light" salvation. They wish to escape hell but do not want to give up fleshly desires and the behavior of an undisciplined lifestyle. Being a *disciple* of Christ means being a "disciplined one." Another term for half-hearted believers is fence-sitters. They want to have one leg on each side of the fence—the best of both worlds. Fence-sitters wish to have their cake and eat it too. They have a place for religion in their lives, but faith is not the base (foundation) their lives are lived from. They are *lukewarm*, as Jesus referred to the Laodicean church.

Overcoming sincere believers who *"follow the Lamb whithersoever he goeth"* do not care about the cost. They sincerely want to serve Jesus as their Master and are not "outlaws" by living in disobedience to His rule. They are not as the Nicolaitane church—adhering to a "salvation" not requiring repentance. "Grace" (effective divine influence) **bears** great fruitfulness in their lives; they listen to and **obey** the Holy Spirit.

Those not voluntarily "losing" their lives as overcomers will physically lose their lives as martyrs. Without loss of life, **either spiritual death to self** or **physical martyrdom** for the name of Jesus, there is **no eternal life** to the soul. That is the everlasting and **greatest loss** of all.

Those grasping the gravity of what is at stake can comprehend significance in the prayer Jesus urged believers to pray. He said, *"Watch ye therefore, and pray always, that ye may be accounted worthy to escape all these things that shall come to pass, and to stand before the Son of Man"* (Luke 21:36). Jesus would not tell believers to pray that specifically for no reason. He meant what He said.

He would not instruct believers to pray to escape future tribulations if it were unnecessary. That instruction indicates all believers—those taken and those left—have choices to make that will affect their lives. Because of God's mercy and love, He sent His Spirit to dwell inside the faithful, strengthening them to be obedient. Jesus said to *"pray always."* Awareness of the Spirit's presence and the fruit He produces will change character. Believers become worthy of the overcomers' place for escape (provision).

Christians have been taught that they may be in a car or an airplane, at work, at school, etc., and then **"Shazam!"** They will suddenly be missing from earth. At that point, the tribulation begins. That scenario is not biblically described. The faithful eagles are gathered at the "carcass" when Jesus returns.

There are **not** two separate raptures—one for the present-day church and another for those who become believers during the tribulation period, as sometimes taught. Only **one** time period is given in Scripture; only **one** rapture is revealed.

By Scripture, certain events **must** occur before Jesus' return and the rapture:

*"Now we beseech you, brethren, by the **coming of our Lord Jesus Christ**, and by our **gathering together to him** [rapture]...³Let **no man deceive you** by any means: for **that day shall not come**, except there come a **falling away first, and** that **man of sin be revealed**, the son of perdition...⁸And then shall that Wicked be revealed, whom the Lord shall consume with the spirit of his mouth, and shall destroy with the brightness of his coming: Even him, whose coming is after the working of Satan with all power and signs and lying wonders, And with all deceivableness of unrighteousness in them that perish; because they received not the love of the truth, that they might be saved. And for this cause God shall send them strong delusion, that they should believe a lie: That they all might be damned who believed not the truth, but had pleasure in unrighteousness."* (2 Thessalonians 2:1, 3, 8-12).

Notice: the Scripture is talking about the Lord's return and **Christians being gathered** to Him (raptured). There **must** be a falling away of the church, **followed by** the **revealing** of the son of perdition (Antichrist). Those events **must** happen **before** the **rapture**. 2 Thessalonians also **substantiates** the chronology presented by this book; the rapture timing corresponds and more Scriptures coincide. The Antichrist is present for the "seven wrath judgments," late in end-time chronology. He is ruling on earth when the rapture occurs.

Jesus corrected His churches early in Revelation, reflecting the "falling away." According to church history, the current era is the only age where female church leadership (the spirit of Jezebel) is an issue. That is a clear indication the **falling away has occurred**. The first seal identified twisted doctrines within the church; that also verifies the falling away. That means the time for provision is getting very close; provision begins before the first beast rises into power.

* * * * *

All Scripture is equally valid as the Word of God! If someone were to begin a wrong interpretation of Scripture, other Scriptures within the Bible would correct the error. God has written His Word in such a way that attentive Christians will not believe error. While giving an interpretation of God's Word, it is of the greatest importance to incorporate **all** the pertinent Scriptures. That will allow the Bible to establish its own interpretation of what it teaches.

Multiple inspired men wrote portions of the material being studied. God's Spirit moved in each one of them to present a uniform, complete history of what will happen **before** it happens; there cannot be **any conflict** between Scriptures. Fulfilled prophecy and the fulfillment of future prophecies prove that the Bible is the Word of God (Isaiah 46:9, 10).

Fleshly nature does not like what is coming upon earth, but God has perfect wisdom. Therefore, the faithful must agree that His plans are best.

Many churches have allowed flawed eschatology to affect other church doctrines. People following their leadership will face problems because of that error. Other **Scriptures conflict** with their doctrines and eschatology; some puzzle pieces of God's Word do not fit together. Bible teachers stretch preferred Scriptures in an attempt to portray and prove what **they want** to believe. As a result, many believers are going to be very confused. They were never taught to pray as Jesus instructed in Luke 21:36, thinking the "sinner's prayer" has them covered. They believe everyone attending their church is saved and will be automatically raptured before conditions get bad on earth; they feel no need to **earnestly pray** and do not realize they **must** get serious about faith. Unfortunately, those may be the ones experiencing the persecutions **they were taught** they **would escape** from. Due to flawed teaching, it is possible some may fall from faith at a time when faith is the only thing left to hold onto.

The truth of God is the truth of God—like it or not! No one gets truth by choosing what he **wants** to believe through emphasizing a few Scriptures that suit his flesh. That is **distorting** God's Word.

These chapters have included a vast amount of Scripture; **all** interlink **without conflict**. Some may still reject this interpretation and believe what they **want** to believe. If such is the case, even God's Word is unable to change their minds (2 Timothy 4:3, 4).

* * * * *

Here is another end-time nugget to uncover from Luke 17:

"In that day, he which shall be upon the housetop, and his stuff in the house, let him not come down to take it away: and he that is in the field, let him likewise not return back. **Remember Lot's wife***"* (vv. 31, 32).

From previous study, some people are "taken" where eagles gather together. Luke 17:31 says there is to be no delay in going; Jesus said to "look up" for redemption. Believers receive instruction in some way—maybe by some sign in the sky, a dream, a vision, or a spiritual visitation. Once received, they are not allowed to return for any provisions. They are to obey! All are told to **remember** Lot's wife. **What was Jesus implying?** Genesis 19:14, *"And Lot went out, and spake unto his sons in law, which **married his***

103

daughters, and said, Up, get you out of this place; for the LORD *will destroy this city. But he seemed as one that mocked unto his **sons in law**.*"

The Bible says Lot, his wife and two **virgin** daughters left the city. God instructed them not to look back. Lot's wife **disobeyed**. *"But his wife looked back from behind him, and she became a pillar of salt"* (v. 26). Lot's wife can easily be criticized for her disobedience, but remember, she had suddenly lost her **married** daughters in a consuming fiery overthrow. Some of **her children** were devoured. Jesus said to remember Lot's wife. He was forewarning believers, there will be a **testing** of **their** obedience; some could fail the test.

Angels came to warn Lot and his family because God considered Lot to be a righteous man. Possibly, the further test of obedience was mainly for his wife and daughters to prove **their** obedience. His wife failed the test; his daughters passed.

All people must heed the warning seen in the example of Lot's family. In Revelation 14:1, if only males are counted in the group of 144,000, their wives and children may also be tested. **All** people must pass the test! When Almighty God speaks, **He requires complete obedience**—no matter how hard it may seem! Jesus is the example for everyone. *"And being found in fashion as a man, he humbled himself, and **became obedient** unto death, even the death of the cross"* (Philippians 2:8).

THE TWO WITNESSES

"And I will give power unto my two witnesses, and they shall prophesy a thousand two hundred and threescore days, clothed in sackcloth...⁶These have power to shut heaven, that it rain not in the days of their prophecy: and have power over waters to turn them to blood, and to smite the earth with all plagues, as often as they will. And when they shall have finished their testimony, the beast that ascendeth out of the bottomless pit shall make war against them, and shall overcome them, and kill them" (Revelation 11:3, 6, 7).

The witnesses will be on earth during the rule of the first beast; he will kill the two men. The time of their appearance is not disclosed. In the Gospels, Jesus indicated there would be a time of persecution of Christians. Those may coincide.

*"For nation shall rise against nation, and kingdom against kingdom: and there shall be famines, and pestilences, and earthquakes in divers places. All these are the beginning of sorrows. **Then** shall they deliver you up to be afflicted, and shall kill you: and ye shall be **hated of all nations** for **my name's sake**"* (Matthew 24:7-9).

The witnesses may be responsible for the famine and pestilences from Matthew 24:7. After those, there will be a worldwide hatred for Christians (v. 9). Luke 21:12-19 confirms public hatred for followers of Christ.

"But before all these, they shall lay hands on you, and

persecute you, delivering you up to the synagogues, and into prisons, being brought before kings and rulers for my name's sake. And it shall turn to you for a testimony. Settle it therefore in your hearts, not to meditate before what ye shall answer: For I will give you a mouth and wisdom, which all your adversaries shall not be able to gainsay nor resist. And ye shall be betrayed both by parents, and brethren, and kinsfolks, and friends; and some of you shall they cause to be put to death. And ye shall be hated of all men for my name's sake. But there shall not a hair of your head perish. In your patience possess ye your souls."

What could be the stimulus for such a vicious hatred and persecution of Christians? Hatred for the two witnesses could be the **catalyst**.

Consider this: if two men professing to be sent by Jesus, cause severe drought, smite the earth with plagues, turn water into blood, and prophesy the judgment of God on the wicked, they will be hated. Consequently, a ripple effect will take place. The hatred people have for the two witnesses will be passed along to everyone believing in Jesus.

According to Revelation 11:7, the two witnesses are killed after completing their mission: *"And when they shall have **finished their testimony**, the beast that ascendeth out of the bottomless pit shall make war against them, and shall overcome them, and **kill them**."* Those two will be so hated that **unbelievers celebrate** their deaths.

> *"And they of the **people** and kindreds and tongues and nations shall **see their dead bodies** three days and a half, and shall **not** suffer their dead bodies **to be put in graves**. And they that dwell upon the earth shall **rejoice** over them,*

106

*and **make merry**, and shall **send gifts** one to another; **because these two prophets tormented them** that dwelt on the earth"* (Revelation 11:9, 10).

According to the passages in Matthew and Luke, Christians will be hated and murdered. They will be perceived as enemies of the world simply because they serve Jesus. The witnesses and martyrs are tied together; **both** are **hated** by the wicked during the end-time.

Even in this escalation of hatred, there is good news. Believers are told not to worry when taken prisoner and brought before judges. **God will tell them** exactly what to say.

*"And it shall turn to you for a **testimony**. Settle it therefore in your hearts, **not to meditate** before what ye shall answer: For **I will give you** a **mouth** and **wisdom**, which all your adversaries shall **not be able** to gainsay nor resist"* (Luke 21:13-15).

Not only will God tell them what to say, their words will be a testimony to all who hear. No one will be able to dispute the truth they testify. *"And this gospel of the kingdom shall be preached in all the world for a **witness unto all** nations; and then shall the end come"* (Matthew 24:14). The testimony of the two witnesses and the end-time saints will fulfill the above prophecy from Matthew. The two witnesses and the end-time testimony of believers are noted again in chapter 14 of Revelation by the first and third angel.

The holy God of love and justice is extending mercy to all who will hear. He will give the end-time Christians the words of **His Truth** so that every soul on earth has an opportunity to believe and be saved from eternal death. God's desire is that **no one** should perish for eternity. He is patient and merciful as described in 2 Peter

3:9, which says, *"The Lord is not slack concerning his promise, as some men count slackness; but is longsuffering to us-ward, **not willing** that any should perish, but that **all should come to repentance.***"

As further testimony of God's great mercy and power, He miraculously brings the two witnesses back to life.

> *"And after three days and an half the **Spirit of life from God entered into them**, and they stood upon their feet; and great **fear fell upon them** which saw them. And they heard a great voice from heaven saying unto them, Come up hither. And they ascended up to heaven in a cloud; and their enemies beheld them"* (Revelation 11:11, 12).

Verse 13 continues, *"And the same hour was there a great earthquake, and the tenth part of the city fell, and in the earthquake were slain of men seven thousand: and the **remnant** were **affrighted**, and **gave glory** to the **God of heaven.***"* Through this calamity, a remnant of people will give glory to God. God uses all situations to continue to reach those who will yield. Every soul makes his own choice as to where he spends eternity. No one will be in heaven or hell by chance. They **deserve** to be at one place or the other. The ability to make that individual choice is all part of the holy justice of God.

The beast from the bottomless pit is not only responsible for killing the two witnesses but will also begin killing the Christian martyrs. Revelation 13:7-10, reveals killing of martyrs **will begin** while the first beast governs the world.

> *"And it was given unto him to make war with the **saints**, and to **overcome them**: and power was given him over all kindreds, and tongues, and nations. And all that dwell upon*

108

*the earth shall worship him, whose names are not written in the book of life of the Lamb slain from the foundation of the world. If any man have an ear, let him hear. **He that leadeth into captivity shall go into captivity: he that killeth with the sword must be killed with the sword. Here is the patience and the faith of the saints.***"*

Some will go into captivity; others will be killed during the fight.

A phrase relating **patience** to believers is also used in Luke 21:19 and Revelation 14:12. It means "death." The first beast will be responsible for the first martyrdoms of Christians fighting against it. They are **not** the sealed and hidden, previously addressed.

Here is a point of interest: though the **first** beast takes over world power, it is not identified by the number "666." The **second** beast carries the 666 identification number. The second is responsible for killing the martyrs taken into captivity.

God knew Christian pacifists will not fight the first beast. Scripture shows they are taken into captivity by the first beast and then later executed by the second beast. The 666 second beast rises three and one-half years after the first beast (Revelation 13:5, 12).

EVENTS IN REVELATION 14

Chapter 14 is an unusual chapter of Revelation; it provides chronology for a number of events, mentioning them through analogies. The context intertwines with events occurring within other chapters. For instance, the testimonies of the two witnesses and martyrs (as mentioned in the previous chapter) will be a worldwide **witness to all people** by an **angel** in chapter 14.

The following sequence brings order to events discovered in other chapters:

1. The sealed 144,000 (vv. 1-5)
2. The testimony of the two witnesses (vv. 6, 7)
3. The fall of Babylon (v. 8)
4. The rise of "666," the second beast (v. 9)
5. The witness of the tribulation martyrs (vv. 9-13)
6. The resurrection of the dead and rapture of the sealed elect (vv. 13-16)
7. The **final** destruction of the wicked (vv. 17-20)

John's second vision of God's wrath (vials) begins in chapter 14. The vision opens with the 144,000 redeemed.

In Revelation 14:6, John sees an angel flying in the midst of heaven. That angel brings the gospel to earth. The manifestation of this angel is accomplished through the **media** broadcasting reports regarding the two witnesses.

An *angel* can be a visible "messenger" appearing as a celestial being; he can also be an invisible messenger affecting the spiritual realm to bring about a physical manifestation. The manifestation makes it appear as though something explainable has occurred.

The "physical" manifestation of "spiritual" events unfolded as the first four seals of Revelation 6 were opened. Each seal released a horseman "spiritually," which brought about a "physical" effect on earth. Those horsemen are unseen by people, even as the angels of chapter 14 are invisible.

The two witnesses from chapter 11 are the "physical" manifestation of the first angel from chapter 14. The angel said, *"Fear God"* and *"the hour of his judgment is come"* (v. 7). The witnesses will prophesy three and one-half years, bringing judgments upon earth and proclaiming truth (the manifestation of the angel's message).

A second angel (v. 8) declares "Babylon has fallen." **Everyone** is affected by the fall and much is to be learned about Babylon when Revelation chapters 17 and 18 are addressed.

The third angel (v. 9) issues a warning **not to take** the mark of the beast. Accepting the mark will ensure God's wrath and eternal destruction. That passage highlights the fact that three and one-half years of the first beast have ended. The **mark** is given by the second beast (Revelation 13:17, 18).

The "physical" manifestation of the third angel is the **testimony** of **captive** martyrs to the entire world. They lay down their lives as **witnesses** to demonstrate that **no one should receive the mark**. Revelation 14:12 says, *"Here is the patience of the saints: here are they that keep the commandments of God, and faith in Jesus."* The phrase *"patience of the saints"* reveals they were faithful to the end.

In the previous chapter, Luke 21:13 was addressed, which says, *"And it shall turn to you for a testimony."* The same Greek word translated *testimony* is **also translated** "witness." Those martyrs are witnesses; they are given wisdom from God that no one is able to refute. That wisdom is for all martyrs around the world (the manifestation of the angel's message).

Next, the earth is "reaped" with a sickle; the first sickle is for the harvest of saints. The first "reaping" (vv. 14-16) is accomplished by the resurrection and rapture. Notice: the **"rapture" matches** where it was presented earlier (after the second beast appears—not pre-tribulation). That is another subtle passage coinciding with the interpretation of this book.

The second sickle throws the *"vine of earth"* (the wicked) into the *"winepress of the wrath of God"* (vv. 17-20). The second group is gathered for destruction. The *"winepress of the wrath of God"* is trodden by **Jesus** during His return (Revelation 19:15).

Both sickles are implemented when the Lord begins His return. The resurrection, rapture and then the wrath of the Lamb are represented by two different sickles harvesting the earth. Both **follow** the second beast which establishes the "mark."

Those events are **represented** in chapter 14 by an **invisible** angel (Revelation 14:19).

A chronology chart in the appendix includes the above sequence as a partial base for other events of Revelation.

Other end-time occurrences are not covered in chapter 14, but they fit together within its framework.

SOCIETY

Scripture needs to be examined in order to observe society **prior** to the rise of the first beast (literally: "dangerous thing").

God wants people to **honor Him** and conduct themselves in the moral manner He approves. God also desires for people to behave kindly, caring for those in genuine need, those unable to help them-selves. The greatest commandments, to love Him first and others next are the important issues to God.

In 2 Timothy 3, God foretold the general attitude of society as the end-time arrives. The following list describes a large portion of today's culture:

> *"For men shall be lovers of their own selves, covetous, boasters, proud, blasphemers, disobedient to parents, unthankful, unholy, Without natural affection, trucebreakers, false accusers, incontinent, fierce, despisers of those that are good, Traitors, heady, high-minded, lovers of pleasures more than lovers of God; Having a form of godliness, but denying the power thereof: from such turn away"* (vv. 2-5).

This nation's current welfare system meets the needs of the poor; it reveals a *"form of godliness"* instituted by a government denying the *"power"* of God. In fact, the liberal side of government would seemingly like to remove **all memory** of God from society.

Truly, people can be seen as lovers of pleasure and things more than God. This nation's media depicts an abundance of inappropriate behaviors and attitudes. Many people imitate the lifestyles and attitudes media has presented.

God's counsel for His people caught up in modern society is

found in Matthew 6:31-33, which say:

*"Therefore take no thought, saying, What shall we eat? or, What shall we drink? or, Wherewithal shall we be clothed? (For after all these things do the Gentiles seek:) for your heavenly Father knoweth that ye have need of all these things. But **seek ye first the kingdom of God, and his righteousness**; and all these things shall be added unto you."*

Seek to please God first; do what is right and let Him direct behavior and decisions made.

The Scriptures are true! God provides for those **sincerely seeking** Him—above reason, above man's wisdom and above personal values.

*"But if from thence thou shalt seek the LORD thy God, thou shalt find him, **if thou seek him with all thy heart** and with **all thy soul**. When thou art in tribulation, and all these things are come upon thee, **even in the latter days**, if thou turn to the LORD thy God, and shalt be **obedient unto his voice** (For the LORD thy God is a merciful God;) he will not forsake thee, neither destroy thee, nor forget the covenant of thy fathers which he sware unto them"* (Deuteronomy 4:29-31).

God's promises are contingent upon **each individual's choice** to come to Him on **His terms**; God said, *"if thou turn"* and *"be obedient."* Man must obey His voice! Notice: the *"latter days"* are addressed. This passage is prophetic in regard to Jesus' calling people to repentance (the seven churches of Revelation). **Trust Him**; He will **do** what His Word proclaims!

114

THE BEASTS

The beasts in Revelation can be very confusing. *Beast* is the word English translators use to convey "dangerous thing" from the Greek language. (Note: the *beasts* at the throne of God are a different Greek word; they are "living things.") In Revelation, there are three "dangerous things" (beasts) to consider and also a dragon.

1) In Revelation 12:3, the dragon is described which metaphorically is Satan (Revelation 20:2).

2) Revelation 17:3, contains the account of a beast that presently carries a "great whore."

3) Revelation 13:1 records a picture of the first beast that **rises** up (*"...a beast rise up out of the sea..."*).

4) Revelation 13:11, 12 explain the second beast that **rises** up (*"...another beast coming up out of the earth..."*).

All four are very closely related because Satan is involved in each. The dragon and the beast that carries the whore (#1 and #2) **both** currently exist but they are spiritual and thereby invisible, only affecting people spiritually. The first and second beasts that **rise** (#3 and #4) become physical and will physically affect people. They are visibly discerned if believers learn how to recognize them.

The dragon's **present** association with the world is explained by chapter 17 where **he** is **portrayed** as a beast (#2). Revelation 12:3 and 17:3 distinguish #1 and #2 respectively; those Scriptures reveal they are one and the same creature; both have seven heads, ten horns, and are red (scarlet). The position of the crowns is noted on the dragon, but not the beast of chapter 17. Forthcoming analysis reveals the beast (#2) currently exists, so the crowns **must** be on his heads, although John didn't note them. Crown position will be addressed shortly. Both of the above spiritual descriptions are invisibly present and apply to the current era.

The dragon (#1, spiritual/unseen, existing now) and the first beast that rises (#3, physical/visibly observed in the future) need to be scrutinized. Their descriptions are very similar and significant because the first **physical** beast (#3) is spiritually **empowered** by the **unseen dragon** (Revelation 13:1, 2).

At this juncture, the **descriptions** for these entities are considered. There is an important difference in appearances; please observe and note the **locations** of crowns.

First, inspect the form of the great red dragon (#1): *"And there appeared another wonder in heaven; and behold a great **red** dragon, having **seven heads** and **ten horns**, and **seven crowns** [diadems] upon his **heads"*** (Revelation 12:3). The crowns are upon the dragon's **heads**. A time period can be identified from Revelation 12:1 and 6; it is from the Old Testament twelve tribes of Israel (twelve stars on her crown) to the time when the woman (God's people) is taken to the wilderness for provision. God's Word shows the dragon exists in that unseen form for a very long time.

The first beast (#3) is described: *"And I stood upon the sand of the sea, and saw a beast **rise** up out of the sea, having **seven heads** and **ten horns**, and upon his **horns ten crowns** [diadems], and upon his heads the name of **blasphemy"*** (Revelation 13:1). The crowns are upon the first beast's **horns**. A *diadem* crown discloses where authority is located.

In Revelation 12:3, the position of the crowns is upon the **heads** of the dragon; that means the place of **authority** is upon his heads. Look again at the portrayal of the first beast (above) in Revelation 13:1. The **crowns have moved** to the horns; in other words, the position of authority has **changed**. The crowns are on the **horns** of the first beast (#3).

Revelation 17 reveals the **unseen** spiritual **beast** (#2), an alias of the dragon (#1), carrying a woman. Revelation 17:3, *"So he carried me away in the spirit into the wilderness: and I saw a*

116

woman sit upon a scarlet-colored [red] *beast, full of names of blasphemy, having seven heads and ten horns.*" (Note: the woman of chapter 17 is **not** the same woman representing God's people from chapter 12. This book's title distinguishes these **two** contrasting women.)

Chapter 17 teaches believers what the beast's **heads** and **horns** represent: *"And here is the mind which hath wisdom. **The seven heads are seven mountains**, on which the woman sitteth"* (Revelation 17:9). The **seven heads** represent **seven mountains**.

What are the horns? *"And the **ten horns** which thou sawest are **ten kings**, which have received **no kingdom as yet...**"* (Revelation 17:12). The **ten horns** represent **ten future kings**.

Scripture has revealed the **heads** are mountains; the **horns** are future kings. Crowns disclose the **location** of authority (government). The **difference** between those two entities (one existing, the other future) is the **location** of government. In Revelation 12:3, government is upon the seven mountains (the heads of the dragon). In Revelation 13:1, the government rests upon the ten kings (the horns of the first beast). The **government has changed**. The diadem crown signifies government. According to Scripture, a huge change is coming for all governments on earth. That change occurs with the physical **rise** of the first beast (#3).

Scripture reveals additional metaphorical description concerning the woman of Revelation 17. *"And the angel said unto me, Wherefore didst thou marvel? I will tell thee the **mystery** of the **woman**, and of the **beast** that **carrieth her**, which hath the **seven heads** and **ten horns**"* (v. 7). The beast (or dragon) is currently supporting this woman, the "great whore." The angel describes those influenced by her, *"And he said unto me, The **waters** which thou sawest where the **whore sitteth**, are **peoples**, and **multitudes**, and **nations**, and **tongues**"* (Revelation 17:15). The "waters" represent all the **people** of earth. The whore is over all people

117

groups; she is depicted as sitting upon people while she is supported by the beast. The whore represents the world's various societies and Satan's influence on people through her.

In review, the beast supports the woman because the woman sits on the beast (v. 3). *"MYSTERY, BABYLON THE GREAT"* yet another name associated with the whore (v. 5), sits on many waters (people, v. 15). The whore represents the abominations of earth (v. 5).

Two matters are hovering over people: the whore represents societies that focus on wickedness. Those societies are supported by the satanic beast, so all people are also exposed to devilish influence from the beast (dragon) supporting the societies.

Verse 9 says, the seven heads are seven mountains (locations) where those societies sit, and **wisdom** is necessary for understanding.

Some students of the Bible believe this passage of Scripture must represent Rome since the woman sits on seven mountains and Rome comprises seven hills. Some have concluded that because Rome is signified, the Pope will be the Antichrist. I do not believe that viewpoint is true. Rome does not rule over leaders all around the globe (v. 18). The Pope has limited, to no influence at all with socialist countries; he does **not rule over** or support them. The "great whore" (v. 1) is above and **corrupts** both the **people** and the **leaders** of **all** the countries on earth **while** supporting them. That explanation does not fit the Pope and Rome.

If verse 9 instructs the reader to exercise wisdom, the answer is not obvious. The whore influences everyone, **corrupting all**, *"With whom the **kings of earth** have committed fornication, and the **inhabitants of the earth** have been made drunk with the wine of her fornication"* (Revelation 17:2). The seven mountains **represent locations** for the "whore" and **all** people.

Instead of Rome's seven hills, consider that there are seven existing mountains that represent a dwelling place for **all** kings and

all people. These mountains are on a larger scale than Rome's seven hills; they are called "continents." Can continents be presented as a **biblical** description for the mountains? **Yes**; this explanation can be found within **Scripture**. When the prophet Jonah was in the belly of the fish, he referred to his location in respect to **mountains**. *"The waters compassed me about, even to the soul: the depth closed me round about, the weeds were wrapped about my head. I went down to the **bottoms of the mountains**..."* (Jonah 2:5, 6).

If Jonah were inside the fish in the depths of the sea and referenced it as being at *"the **bottoms of the mountains**,"* then **tops** of mountains rising above the sea are dry land where people can live. Globally, the earth has seven mountains rising **above the sea** called continents. The seven mountains of Revelation 17 represent the **seven continents** of earth. "Wisdom" is needed; this **scripturally** acceptable interpretation makes sense with the related verses.

To recap: the seven heads for both beasts (#2, #3) and the dragon are metaphors for the seven continents of earth. The horns on top of the heads represent **future** leaders for all countries. The **location** of the crowns represents the beast's current location of government (presently on the heads, in the future on the horns). The whore represents wicked societies that developed with support and influence from the devil. The societies' governments are over the people, depicted by the whore sitting on the waters, representing all people; thus, she is over **all** inhabitants of earth.

Societies are currently **supported** by the beast (dragon). The government is presently upon the continents (heads); that represents the "law of the land." The crowns move to the ten future kings (horns) when governments are changed.

A NEW SYSTEM

Revelation 17:3 and 12, disclose the ten horns of the beast represent ten kings **not yet in power**. They are established when the first beast governs earth. The crowns move when the spiritual dragon empowers the physical first beast (Revelation 13:2). That is why the descriptions for those creatures are the same, excepting the **location** of crowns. This world's presently existing societies are supported by the spiritually invisible dragon.

For a new government to come into place, old authorities must be displaced. The crowns must move; they will not co-exist. How could that displacement occur?

The seven-headed, ten-horned red dragon from Revelation 12, pre-existed Jesus' birth (vv. 3-5); it was probably established after the Great Flood. A guess is that it took form after the Tower of Babel and continues to exist to present day. (Detailing as to "why" is unnecessary.) At present, ruling authorities for people of earth are upon the "heads," i.e., the mountains—the continents. In today's dialect, the governing bodies for countries are the "**law of the land.**" Governments for the various countries are different. In the language of Revelation, the crowns of authority are on the dragon's heads.

Keep in mind, the beast of chapter 17 **supports** all of the kings (leaders) and people of earth. The governing system supporting Babylon the Great existed in Jesus' time. Crowns were on the heads then and remain in place today. The whore, Mystery Babylon, is **still** supported by the **same** dragon/beast (Revelation 17:3, 7). The governing crowns remain the "law of the land."

In Revelation 12, war takes place in heaven; Satan (the dragon) is cast down to earth (vv. 7-9). When Satan is cast into earth from heaven (a significant change), it makes sense the crowns will

120

move. Satan will no longer have access to God so that He can accuse believers (Revelation 12:10). War in heaven is the spiritual catalyst for the physical rise of the first beast.

A new governing system is coming. As already stated, the old governing system must be displaced by the new system. In fact, because the new system hates the old system, Mystery Babylon is completely destroyed.

The first beast of Revelation 13:1 establishes government through **his ten kings** (horns). During the rule of the first beast, traditional governments as currently known (the law of the land by sovereignty of countries) are ended. That is how seven crowns become ten crowns. In John's visions, they only locate government.

*"And the **ten horns** which thou sawest upon the beast, **these shall hate the whore**, and shall make her desolate and naked, and shall eat her flesh, and burn her with fire"* (Revelation 17:16). In biblical language to *burn with fire,* means to completely destroy. Nothing is left from the old governing systems. The whore, representing societies existing with governing and financial systems throughout the earth, is completely destroyed by ten future kings.

Whenever I hear the term "New World Order," my internal alarm bell goes off. The beast of Revelation 13 may currently be preparing to rise.

The *whore* represents governing and financial systems and societies that currently exist. Presently, cultures contain people who cheat and lie; they are immoral, selfish, greedy and materialistic. The whore involves the **leaders** and **all classes** of people. Every governing system has an associated financial system; it is small wonder that the leaders and people carry out wickedness for financial gain.

Satan (the dragon's power [Revelation 20:2]) is supporting fornication (immorality and greed), by urging people to be

121

discontent and seek to obtain more pleasures and lusts.

How is the **desire** for **more** corrupt in God's eyes?

"But godliness with contentment is great gain. For we brought nothing into this world, and it is certain we can carry nothing out. And having food and raiment let us be therewith content. But they that will be rich fall into temptation and a snare, and into many foolish and hurtful lusts, which drown men in destruction and perdition. For the love of money is the root of all evil: which while some coveted after, they have erred from the faith, and pierced themselves through with many sorrows" (1 Timothy 6:6-10).

Being pleasure-minded is the focus of many today, getting bigger, nicer, better belongings. Most Christians do not consider how they can become more Christ-like in character and glorify God (John 15:8). Not many live in contentment by God's standards. They don't take time to contemplate God's Word; instead, they ponder how to get ahead. Many still participate in the great whore's greed, materialism and self-indulgence—even in the church. Through grace, anyone is able to overcome. Cooperate with the Holy Spirit; He is the power of God **in** you. All that Satan is able to do right now is "tempt" people. He will personify later with much greater power to deceive (2 Thessalonians 2:8-11).

The *whore*, Mystery Babylon, is the first of another doubled-vision. John is **called to the angel** (heaven is their abode) in Revelation 17:1. Then in Revelation 18:1, an angel comes **down from** heaven as John watches from **earth's** vantage point. The two visions are different perspectives but both concern the same subject, Mystery Babylon.

The whore of chapter 17, is identical to "Babylon the great" in chapter 18. Each chapter provides a description of Babylon. In chapter 17, John is watching from heaven; that indicates the wording he employs is metaphorical as he looks at the beast and whore.

In chapter 18, subjects are physical, actual people i.e., kings (leaders), merchants, shipmasters (transportation corporations), sailors, musicians, and craftsman exhibiting the luxurious abundance of Babylon. *"And I heard another voice from heaven, saying, Come out of her, my people, that ye be not partakers of her sins, and that ye receive not of her plagues"* (Revelation 18:4). This **Scripture** reveals that Jesus' church exists **within** the **whore**. His plea is for His people to repent and come out of her. His correction to His people in Revelation 18:4 is paralleled in the correction He gave to the seven churches. Please consider and search your heart. Are you caught up in the desires of the "whore"—materialism, pleasure, greed, discontentment, getting ahead, immorality? If so, *"come out of her"* and **repent**!

Reading chapter 18 is recommended. Notice: the rulers, merchants and those transporting the woman's goods all mourned her destruction because she was so lavish. In other words, they live through her destruction but mourn because of losing their former means of wealth.

Revelation 18:17, *"...in **one hour** so great riches is come to nought...."* That phrase is extremely significant; it is *"one hour"* that the ten kings of the beast reign together and **hate** the whore (Revelation 17:12, 13). "One hour" is the common time period in each vision (probably not a literal hour since many metaphors are used). It undoubtedly indicates the time encompassing governmental change-over is surprisingly short. The ten future kings reign (chapter 17), and Babylon is to be destroyed (chapter 18) in one hour. That is not coincidental.

It should be noted that though the time to **establish** a new governing system may be brief, the first beast is in power for forty-two months (v. 5), that is, three and one-half years. That era establishes the physical governing of the first beast. Later, the second beast will emerge, adding absolute religious authority. Governmental and religious authorities will belong to Satan when he personifies within the second beast.

God **doubles** judgment upon Babylon, according to Revelation 18:6. Once something is demolished the first time, it is terminated. How can total destruction be doubled? Satan supports the *great whore* alias *Babylon the great* (society). After the *whore* is obliterated through governmental change, Satan will support a different global governing system and society. That one is also destined for abolishment when Jesus returns. The destruction of wicked societies and their governments happens twice: the *great whore* governed by seven crowns, and the *government of the beast* with ten crowns. At the end of this age, all former crowns of authority will belong to Jesus during the millennial reign; that is the description John employed for his vision of Jesus when returning as KING OF KINGS AND LORD OF LORDS, *"...and on his head were **many** crowns..."* (Revelation 19:12). The Scriptures faultlessly fit together.

A possibility of how modern-day governments could change is presented next: the rise of the first beast is possible in this current era.

THE FIRST BEAST

Speculations contained in this chapter are conjecture, but indeed have a potential for becoming reality. The chapters concerning the first and second beasts that rise are portions of this book that are purely logical guesses. In spite of considerable evidence, whether or not this evaluation of evidence is true is another matter.

Currently, at the writing of this book, the Presidential election of 2016 has awarded President Donald Trump the victory. A "war" in heaven is being waged and the "dragon" lost a battle. It should become evident this battle only delays the first beast's rise to power. The recent victory represents a reprieve and allows the faithful more time to develop in righteousness and do the work God has called them to.

Take a closer look at the first beast ("dangerous thing"): *"And the beast which I saw was like unto a leopard, and his feet were as the feet of a bear, and his mouth as the mouth of a lion: and the dragon gave him his power, and his seat, and great authority"* (Revelation 13:2).

The first beast was *"like unto a leopard."* For what attributes would a leopard be noted? One of the most significant traits is **stealth**, its hunting tactic. **It sneaks up unobserved on its prey**. Could there be entities that are not obvious but yet able to change the world's governments and financial systems? Please do an internet search; read about the organizations listed. These are not normally considered powerful to most people because they are obscure. Please search and read from several sources about the Bilderberg Group, the Council on Foreign Relations, and the Trilateral Commission.

Each of the organizations mentions a **target** of obtaining "one-world government." Statements by leaders such as David Rockefeller and Richard Haass are **treasonous** against the sovereignty of independent countries. If you haven't read about them, please do so. They could remove references to "one-world government" should that become an issue.

Take notice of the connected leaderships establishing those organizations and the influence of Mr. Brzezinski. They also share interests with the World Bank. They have an objective of **world peace**. Look at what Daniel says about the end-time ruler: *"...and by peace shall destroy many..."* (Daniel 8:25). How can peace be used as a weapon to destroy? The prophecy fits together with the goals of the above organizations. That is not accidental. I do not want to be labeled a conspiracy theorist, but those organizations are bold, voluntarily making statements of what they are working toward since conception.

In 1990 President George H. Bush mentioned a "new world order" in some of his speeches. What did he mean? Many U.S. Presidents' cabinets have included people from the above-listed organizations, particularly the Council on Foreign Relations. Former President Obama had eleven members on his staff. Many presidential staff people had a "one-world government" agenda to work toward while they influenced policies for the existing government.

Those organizational members serve a global agenda not visible to the general public. Their attitude is beginning to emerge to the public eye. They are globalist; there is no loyalty to any nation. That is why they promote the liberal vs. conservative conflicts in this country. They don't care about the country; they want to divide it. People with a global agenda have been shaping governmental decisions for the United States and would like to remove the Constitution. Does that sound comparable to a leopard's stealthy approach within government? (President Trump is trying to

126

serve the **nation**; he is being referred to as a "nationalist.")

Additional description is given for the first beast in Revelation 13:2, *"…and his feet were as the feet of a bear.…"* A bear uses its feet as its primary weapon to fight, obliterating an opponent or article. Its claws rip and tear things to pieces. That description characterizes what the ten future kings of the first beast do to "Mystery Babylon" (the whore from chapters 17 and 18); they destroy **everything** pertaining to the whore.

Revelation 13:7 continues: *"And it was given unto him to make war with the **saints**, and to **overcome** them: and **power** was given him **over all** kindreds, and tongues, and nations."* He is permitted to have power everywhere and **overcome** the **immature** believers not under God's provision.

"…and his mouth as the mouth of a lion…" (Revelation 13:2). The lion is known for the **volume** of his **roar**; no one shouts louder or is more persuasive. The beast opens his mouth to speak against God, *"And he opened his mouth in blasphemy against God, to blaspheme his name, and his tabernacle, and them that dwell in heaven"* (Revelation 13:6).

In modern language, this "dangerous thing" controls **professional mass media** (the mouth of a lion). Its influence covers all media: movies, television, magazines, newspapers, radio and internet. Influencing those venues allows the beast to **shape** the **attitudes** of people. All communications are biased and continually presenting the beast's attitude and viewpoint. The viewpoints and people the beast doesn't like are degraded, only his favored standpoints are promoted. In essence, people are effectively brainwashed into having an attitude the beast wants them to have. God and Christians are continually presented in mocking and unbecoming scenarios.

Since Satan gives the beast power, people will not hear anything good about the Christian faith. The "attitude" of how faith

127

is presented is negatively biased. God is blasphemed; those who believe in Him are also demeaned.

That development is to be expected. Consider how media (especially movies and television shows) has degraded and mocked sincere Christian faith for many years. This degradation will only get worse—much worse **after** the first beast is in power.

Please look at membership lists of the organizations mentioned in this chapter. The CEOs of mass media are well-represented as members within those assemblies. The mouth of the lion is already established in this world; the media is prepared for the beast to use its influence.

The globalist elite do not realize they are Satan's tool, being used to obtain **his objectives**. They believe they established ideals and goals to benefit humanity. Unfortunately, human knowledge often opposes God (Isaiah 47:10).

The following quote is taken from *Time* magazine involving the 2016 election. This secular magazine has unknowingly but correctly described biblical prophecy for the end-time. It describes the rise of "knowledge" (Daniel 12:4), and a "beast" that people ride on while not perceiving its danger (Revelation 17:7).

What does it mean to put a computer in the palm of every human being, and to link each palm instantaneously with every other? When Gutenberg's revolution of movable type first made it possible to share ideas widely across space and time, the political and social follow-on effects included the Reformation, the Enlightenment, the rise of democracy and the industrial and scientific revolutions. In other words, everything from daily routines to international order was scrambled and re-scrambled. How much change, and how rapid, will this massively more powerful technology cause? Elites have been riding high on the back of this beast, and have not yet seen its teeth or felt its claws. But many millions more Americans, living outside of the best zip codes, feel it breathing down their necks.

Time; November 21, 2016 p.36

128

Through **finances** the first beast can rise into power, overcoming the present governments. Each country has its own central bank. The Federal Reserve Bank of the United States of America is **not** part of the government of the United States. It is **not** under the authority of the United States Department of Treasury. It is a **private** banking entity. The **only** influence the United States government has, is to appoint its CEO when needed. Aside from that limited control, the Federal Reserve Bank is **independent** of **all governmental control**. In other words, present society is supported by (rides on) a privately controlled financial system. **All** leaders and **every** citizen work under that financial system to buy homes, food, clothes, and have the pleasures of living life. The same is true for other countries of the world. That description **corresponds** to the great whore (peoples, multitudes, nations, and tongues) riding upon the beast (chapter 17).

The World Bank and national central banks are powers that go unnoticed, yet **all** people are **supported** by them. Their existence is centered on money; it is easy to see how corruption takes place with both leaders and citizens.

No governmental agency oversees banks. The financiers in charge do as they please. Banks distribute money as **they** see fit—**without accountability to anyone**. The old cliché, "money is power," is certainly true. Debt is throughout the world; banks have power everywhere. They create it and distribute it. **Governments** around the globe are in **debt** to those **private** banking systems. Who can guess the influence/power those systems gain as countries dig deeper and deeper into debt every year. The high-level bank officers in Freddie Mac and Fannie Mae all received their salaries and bonuses even though the banking institutions went bankrupt. They were paid by U.S. tax payers. Congress wouldn't stop it. WHY not? The U.S. government yielded to the influence of high-level financiers. That is only **one** instance that almost everyone knows about. What other pressures do financiers exert throughout the world to achieve their global goals?

It does not take insight to see the power of **banking institutions** increasing. Financiers set interest rates according to their own will. A good guess is that the global elite will choose to fight President Trump by raising interest rates to injure the economy before the next election. If citizens are hurt financially, they are more likely to choose a different president in three years. Globalists want one of "their people" in the White House so they can implement policies that will wreck this country financially through debt, and loss of jobs to foreign countries.

Economies around the globe are more interdependent than ever. If a major country's economy crashes, more will follow. When that happens, banks will declare the present governments **bankrupt**; they have no ability to pay their vast, escalating debt. At that point, unregulated banking systems will **own** governments of countries. Banks will literally repossess or foreclose on the leadership of countries through the medium of finances. (That is when the crowns move from the heads to horns in John's visions.)

Perhaps that is why policies made by former leaders and staffs drove the United States ever deeper into debt. **Debt**, a **weapon** that promoters of one-world government use, comes as a Trojan horse and infiltrates a nation.

When a home or a business is foreclosed, any equity is totally lost. The same will apply to governments. The next system described in Revelation will not retain anything from the former system (Revelation 17:16). **Banks** will then establish a **world governing** system through organizations **they** have worked with and intermingled leadership with. (Those listed at the beginning of this chapter.)

The implementation of the *amero,* a new currency printed for use in Mexico, the United States and Canada will probably occur. It is the equivalent to the *euro* currently used in Europe but hasn't been implemented. Look it up to verify it for yourself. (There is some debate about its authenticity. Search "amero currency" and look at Snopes.com and HalTurnerShow.com. Decide what you believe.) If a new financial system is started, the present currency will be useless because it is part of a bankrupt system. The necessary instruments for a great change are coming into place.

The first beast will physically rise up out of the "sea" of mankind (Revelation 13:1). The beast is a **group** of human leaders (ten future kings). This group will project liberal views because it is spiritually empowered by Satan (Revelation 13:2). That is why liberals currently fight this country's conservative Christian foundations.

Previous monarchies and dynasties came to an end, allowing the *seed of men* (upcoming study) to gain positions of authority. For people not attentive to the coming change, it will look as though the **style** of **government** changes when the beast rises. That "rise" is the globalist agenda.

Globalists have greatly influenced younger generations by swaying educational values in the schools and colleges. Countless younger Americans have been "brainwashed" into a different "base value" for thinking by educational institutions. By perspective, they are *secular progressives.* Through rejecting God, they focus on values based in "humanism." Those ideologies conflict with the traditional founding principles of this land, thus producing the notably occurring division.

Along with abandonment of God **disguised** as "separation of church and state," there is no appreciation for U.S. history that would inspire patriotism. The result is that precious few young people value this country and the many individuals who fought and died making and keeping it free.

Children are being influenced in school systems through

both curriculum and teachers that express the liberal agenda, camouflaged in academics. Liberals have motivated a lot of social change in favor of their side through educational manipulation. (Example: removing U.S. history to eventually promote globalism.) If you have children, educate them to understand what liberals stand for. Home schooling or private Christian schools are possible alternatives to protect children from the subtle brainwashing occurring in many public school systems. If public school is the only option, involve as many other parents as possible and as a group express disapproval for modern curriculum changes. As a unit, demand that schools teach the history of the United States, Constitution, Bill of Rights and the founding fathers' acknowledgment of God being written into its documents.

Secular progressives divide the people of this nation with modern liberal vs. traditionally conservative viewpoints; they promote the liberal side. The battle between those opposing ideologies has become very clear in light of the past election year. Citizens should now understand "far right" and "far left" have extremely differing value systems.

The news reports and articles that liberals influence keep exacerbating **dissension** between citizenry concerning every possible contentious subject. They promote divisive attitudes between people groups across the land by giving significant news coverage to disputable topics and events. Quarrelsome opinions become headline news. Nothing good or unifying is given that status; the result is general discontentment across the land, brainwashing. Citizens lose their appreciation for what this country **offers**—freedom and opportunity. Instead, the focus is on every negative factor. The news media presents disapproval toward those who lead with traditional values. Criticisms are always the focus. News is not simply reported; negative opinion and bias is included in its coverage.

Unity is broken so that through annoyance in the citizens, something different... globalism, can emerge. Jesus said, "...*Every kingdom divided against itself is brought to desolation; and every city or house divided against itself shall not stand*" (Matthew 12:25). A cliché even exists within the secular realm, "divide and conquer." When liberal views are presented, the dividing of the nation is being promoted. Their promoted, liberal ideology fights traditional values and creates the division. Those communicating liberal ideology are the ones **promoting** and **promulgating** division. If possible, boycott them! Do not consume their goods or services; cease listening to or watching those stations or buying those magazines and papers. Christian stations and publications report news that is important. (In the secular realm, Fox News appears to be the least biased at present.) Stop patronizing retailers that promote the liberal agenda. Christian organizations such as the American Family Association (AFA.NET) can identify those retailers. Christians can financially fight against the liberal agenda through boycotts. If Christians tell all friends and family members to boycott, money can be a powerful weapon used against the spread of liberalism. Social media can be an influential tool.

Liberals pushed for laws to "gag" the church from expressing support for political candidates with conservative ideals (the "Johnson Law" of 1954). That law effectively removed "conservative church" influence from elections. Financially, they intimidated the church with the threat of losing its tax exemption; it worked. Political candidates with Christian values were not endorsed by churches. Christians can use that same weapon of *finances* to fight against news organizations, Hollywood and businesses supporting the liberal agenda.

Christian values have been under attack and believers are **forced** into a political/social war. Don't surrender without putting up a good fight; **do something!** This country was founded on **God's**

133

principles; the **change** liberals promote cannot be for the better.

The United States as we know it is in a struggle for **survival**. If liberal globalists win the war to control the United States, this country and the world will never be the same again. A global hierarchy will never again allow "government of the people, by the people and for the people." Uniting their financial monarchy with the unmatched military might of the United States, they will be unstoppable from subduing all nations.

Perhaps there is some merit to the conspiracy theory; what do **you think** is happening in this country?

The strategies globalists use against other countries need to be investigated further. Only tactics used against the United States are identified in this writing.

Current events are the result of **spiritual influences** no one can see. As the unity of this nation decays, the stage is being set for a coming major change.

At present, the whore (the present governments, finances and societies) continues to be supported by the dragon (Satan), **until** power is given to the first beast. The **physical manifestation** initiating the first beast is the bankruptcy of existing governments. Bankrupting nations (the fall of Babylon) is the catalyst moving the crowns.

Spiritually, the rise of the first beast is the result of a war when Satan (the dragon) is cast out of heaven (Revelation 12:9). The **time** for **warfare** in **heaven** is current; it manifests on earth in the form of the leopard's **stealthy approach** (globalists using debt to devise bankrupting of nations). Reiterating that, the bankrupting of nations **causes** Babylon's fall; it is the **physical** manifestation on earth of a **spiritual** war in heaven.

Once Satan has world-controlling power through the first beast, his ten leaders assure total destruction of this "present world order" (the whore of Revelation 17 and 18). Through the ten kings of the first beast, Satan (as the dragon) will destroy the former system that he once supported and influenced.

Enormous riches rapidly disappear according to chapter 18. The new system will own everything. Just like foreclosure on a home or business, the equity that was paid will be worthless; all the former wealth and ownership within the bankrupt system disappears.

Many people, including believers, will fight to keep what was theirs under the old system. In patriotism, they will fight for their former governments and freedoms the first beast takes away. In faith, they fight against the beast that blasphemes God. They will fight as their forefathers also fought for freedom. Though they fight, this time they will all lose, including Christians, *"...he that killeth with the sword must be killed with the sword. Here is the patience of the saints"* (Revelation 13:10). Those will be **immature** servants of God fighting, one reason why the number of martyrs is vast (Revelation 7:9). Unfortunately, the first beast has total victory all around the globe. *"And a mighty angel took up a stone like a great millstone, and cast it into the sea, saying, Thus **with violence** shall that great city **Babylon** be thrown down, and shall be found no more at all"* (Revelation 18:21).

After global governmental change, unrest continues, *"And I saw one of his heads as it were wounded to death; and his deadly wound was healed: and all the world wondered after the beast"* (Revelation 13:3). Many think this passage means a human leader receives a fatal head injury and comes back to life. That interpretation is not accurate. Recall the **scriptural** interpretation for the "heads" of the beast. The heads represent **mountains**, and the mountains represent continents. A **huge geological area** will receive a wound. Only a weapon of mass destruction could be used against a continent. The wound of that weapon is deadly, but it doesn't produce death: *"...his deadly wound was healed."* It may be a nuclear attack against an entire region of the world; however, that attack is ineffective to kill anyone.

The next verse contains the logical, human nature response to be expected. People said, *"...Who is like unto the beast? Who is able to make **war** with him"* (Revelation 13:4)? They experience the natural reaction of awe and **fear** of the **world power**. Consider this: it would **not** seem impossible to make *"war"* against **one leader**, one person receiving a head wound that was healed.

Revelation 13:4 also displays that the ten future kings destroying the whore will **not** produce world peace. They are able to destroy the remnants of democracy, socialism, communism, and dictatorships. They make all people citizens of a new world order, but wars and unrest among people groups continues.

Revelation 13:7 indicates the first beast overcomes the saints of God. That is confirmed within John's visions, Revelation 12:17, *"And the dragon was wroth with the woman, and went to **make war** with the remnant of her seed, which keep the commandments of God, and have the testimony of Jesus Christ."* That is speaking of the **immature seed** of the woman. The woman (spiritually mature overcomers/church) is carried to the wilderness and hidden.

Consider when martyrdoms occur: the first beast kills the two witnesses (Revelation 11:7). Some saints die fighting the first beast (Revelation 13:10); those are also viewed making war in chapter 12. Other saints will go into captivity.

The pacifists of the Christian faith do not believe in fighting and are taken captive by the first beast. Revelation 6:11 and 20:4, reveal the captives are killed by the second beast, *"He that leadeth **into captivity** shall go **into captivity**: he that **killeth** with the sword **must be killed** with the sword. Here is the **patience** and the **faith** of the **saints**"* (Revelation 13:10). The *patience and the faith of the saints* confirm martyrdom.

SATAN, THE BEAST OF 17

"And the angel said unto me, Wherefore didst thou marvel?
*I will tell thee the mystery of the woman, and of the **beast***
*that carrieth her, which hath **seven heads and ten horns**.*
*The **beast** that thou sawest **was**, and **is not**; and **shall ascend***
*out of the bottomless pit, and **go into perdition**: and they*
that dwell on the earth shall wonder, whose names were not
written in the book of life from the foundation of the world,
*when they behold the **beast** that **was**, and **is not**, and **yet is** "*
(Revelation 17:7, 8).

A beast which *"was, is not, yet is, shall ascend, and go into*
perdition," is the topic of a difficult riddle to comprehend.
Examining the verses one phrase at a time will bring understanding.

The beast in this passage supports Mystery Babylon (the
whore) from chapter 17. The beast has the same description as
Satan in Revelation 12:3. (No crowns are present, which only
identify where government is located.) This beast represents the
power of Satan in society (his spiritual influence). The riddle-like
passage is about Satan's **power** and the **changes** that occur to his
power in dealing with humans. These descriptions are spiritual, not
physical; they metaphorically reveal what is happening in the
spiritual world. Examining his changes according to **Scripture**,
allows God's Word to disclose how this riddle is to be understood.

"Wherein in time past ye walked according to the course of
*this world, according to the **prince of the power of the air**, the spirit*
that now worketh in the children of disobedience" (Ephesians 2:2).
From when Adam and Eve disobeyed God, sin ruled and reigned in
the hearts of men. Satan was *"the prince of the power of the air."*
His power and authority on earth were truly established; otherwise,

he could **not** have tempted Jesus.

> *"And the **devil**, taking him up into a high mountain, showed unto him all the kingdoms of the world in a moment of time. And the **devil** said unto him, all this power **will I give** thee, and the glory of them: for **that is delivered unto me**; and to **whomsoever I will I give it**. If thou therefore wilt worship me, all shall be thine. And Jesus answered and said unto him, Get thee behind me, Satan: for it is written, Thou shalt worship the Lord thy God, and him only shalt thou serve"*
> (Luke 4:5-8).

This Scripture proves that Satan *"was"* in authority power over the seven continents. In view of that passage, the dragon was described as having seven crowns of authority upon his heads (continents) in Revelation 12:3. He **supports** the world's societies and their governments; they "ride" on him and he encourages them in all the traits of the whore. In prior history, physical authority was through monarchies. At present, he doesn't care if a country is democratic, socialist/communist, or a dictatorship; he promotes the sinful nature of people living within its boundaries. According to the riddle, Satan *"was."*

Revelation states that he *"is not."* The victory in the cross of Jesus, overcame the power Satan received. He is no longer *"the prince of the power of the air"* (sin). **Anyone** willing to call upon Jesus can be delivered from Satan's reduced power. Although the whore exists, Satan does not have power to bind people to her.

> *"And the seventy returned again with joy, saying, Lord, even the devils are subject unto us through thy name. And he said unto them, I beheld **Satan** as lightning **fall** from heaven. Behold, I give you power to tread on serpents and*

138

*scorpions, and **over all the power of the enemy**: and nothing shall by any means hurt you"* (Luke 10:17-19).

The people who follow Christ are freed from Babylon (the whore). They have *"come out of her"* (Revelation 18:4). Through Jesus, man can escape Satan. Now he *"is not."*

The riddle says he "was," "is not," *"yet is"*; he remains present but without power over everyone. He still supports the whore and rules over unregenerate people within her, but he only has ability to **tempt** the faithful (1 Thessalonians 3:5). He does **not** have **authority** beyond **tempting** believers with faith in Christ. (If you are a Christian, the devil didn't **make** you do it!) His power is much greater in those **not** belonging to God. Humans serve either God or sin (Satan). Jesus paid the full price for people to be saved, healed, delivered, and provided for. He gave them power (His Spirit) to live in obedience to God by grace.

Jesus is currently saving souls; He made reference to when Satan will rise into power again. *"I must work the works of him that sent me, while it is day: **the night cometh, when no man can work**"* (John 9:4). This verse is an indication for when the **second** beast **physically** and **spiritually** governs earth. There is no biblical evidence that people continue to be saved during that time.

According to 2 Thessalonians 2:3, Satan personifies physically and visibly, not simply spiritually as in the past (*"prince of the power of the air"*). He is portrayed, *"**coming up** out of the earth"* (Revelation 13:11) to be a portion of the second beast. That physical manifestation is confirmed by the riddle in Revelation 17:8, saying he *"...**shall ascend** out of the bottomless pit...."* He ascends into physical, global authority.

In the riddle, Satan's final destiny is to *"**go into perdition**"* (Revelation 17:8). An upcoming second riddle concerning "seven kings," concludes with an eighth king who also *"goeth into*

139

perdition" (Revelation 17:11). The final destiny (perdition) verifies a common outcome and identity for the eighth king.

The riddle of "seven kings" is addressed in Revelation 17:10 and 11; the conclusion and explanation of that riddle leads right back to Satan's **physical** rising (the second beast), when **he** becomes the eighth king. The following verses reveal how the two riddles relate:

> *"And here is the mind which hath **wisdom**. The seven heads are seven mountains, on which the woman sitteth. And **there are seven kings: five are fallen, and one is, and the other is not yet come**; and when he cometh, he must **continue a short space**. And the beast that **was, and is not**, even he is the **eighth** and is **of the seven**, and goeth into **perdition"*** (Revelation 17:9-11).

The seven mountains are the seven continents on which people live—the landmasses of earth. This Scripture mentions seven authorities (kings). This riddle could be easily misunderstood by thinking that a "king" will come from each continent; however, that supposition would not be accurate because an "eighth king" will come; there are not eight continents. Instead, specific eras of "governing" on the seven continents are the focus of this passage. Notice how the Scripture reads: *"five are fallen* (they are past), *and one is* (only one exists now), *and the other is not yet come"* (one is in the future). Continents have not *"fallen"*; the leadership on them has. The Scripture is speaking of the total time period from the **beginning to end** of governmental rule on earth by men. A **total** of **seven governments** by men are recognized by God; then afterward, the eighth government by Satan (*beast that was, and is not*) will be directly related to one of the seven kings (government by men).

Who or what might those seven kings or authorities be

140

according to Scripture? God clarifies most of this information in the dream of Nebuchadnezzar. Daniel's interpretation of that dream reveals that God was referring to kings/authorities upon earth in the past, present and future.

"This image's head was of fine gold, his breast and arms of silver, his belly and his thighs of brass, His legs of iron, his feet part of iron and part of clay. Thou sawest till that a stone was cut out without hands, which smote the image upon his feet that were of iron and clay, and broke them to pieces. Then was the iron, the clay, the brass, the silver, and the gold, broken to pieces together, and become like the chaff of the summer threshing floors; and the wind carried them away, that no place was found for them: and the stone that smote the image became a great mountain, and filled the whole earth" (Daniel 2:32-35).

In the book of Daniel, Nebuchadnezzar's kingdom is represented as the "head of gold." By widely accepted history, the Medes and Persians were the "silver chest and arms;" the Greeks and Macedonians were the "brass belly and thighs;" the Romans were represented by the "legs of iron." These can be studied in greater depth in chapters 7 and 8 of Daniel. Even **if** the respective above conclusions are in error, God has only revealed a **total** of **five** authorities by that dream.

The biblical passages are metaphorical, but accurate. Secular historians not acknowledging divine inspiration maintain the Book of Daniel must have been written **after** those kingdoms fell, because of its historical accuracy. (**They** don't believe that God could foretell the future.)

"And as the toes of the feet were part of iron, and part of

141

*clay, so the kingdom shall be partly strong, and partly broken. And whereas thou sawest iron mixed with miry clay, they shall **mingle** themselves with the **seed of men**: but they shall not cleave one to another, even as iron is not mixed with clay. And **in the days of these kings** shall the God of heaven **set up a kingdom, which shall never be destroyed**: and the kingdom shall not be left to other people, but it shall break in pieces and consume all these kingdoms, and it shall stand forever. Forasmuch as thou sawest that the stone was cut out of the mountain without hands, and that it broke in pieces the iron, the brass, the clay, the silver, and the gold; the great God hath made known to the king what shall come to pass hereafter: and the dream is certain, and the interpretation thereof sure"* (Daniel 2:42-45).

The phrase *"iron mixed with miry clay"* will soon be addressed in greater depth, but the first four authorities from Nebuchadnezzar's dream must be considered. According to Revelation 17, **five** kings (authorities) are **fallen**. A **total** of only **five** authorities are revealed through Nebuchadnezzar. Daniel and Revelation are not a perfect match; one authority is missing from Daniel.

If *"iron mixed with miry clay"* represents current governments, then **only four authorities are left** from Nebuchadnezzar's dream. Somewhere in Scripture, God must have revealed the **fifth fallen** authority. The riddle says *"five are fallen."* God has revealed another authority by **Scripture**; He never said much about that fallen authority, but Revelation 16 makes mention of it: *"And the sixth angel poured out his vial upon the great river Euphrates; and the water thereof was dried up, that the way of the **kings** of the east might be prepared"* (v. 12). The dynasty governments of the East (the Orient) have **fallen**. They may represent **the fifth** of the fallen kingdoms, those whose **governing**

142

period in **history** has **ended.**

Revelation 17's *"the kingdom that is"* needs to be identified. In Nebuchadnezzar's dream, that kingdom is *"iron mixed with miry clay,"* and *"they shall* **mingle themselves** *with the seed of men"* (Daniel 2:43). In today's world governments, there is no longer a royal lineage for succession of power, as in prior history. Nations are divided by basic ruling standards of democracy, socialism, communism, or military dictatorship, none of which have birth lineage for royalty and succession. The kingdoms of today are **truly mixed** with *"the seed of men"*; there is **no regard** for bloodlines. Today's kingdoms are all separate; some are strong, and some are weak. The description flawlessly fits **current** societies. **Existing governments** represent the **sixth** authority of Revelation 17:10—that which now *"is."*

"...and **the other is not yet come;** *and when he cometh, he must* **continue a short space"** (Revelation 17:10). The different authorities that were previously referred to prevailed for many years. The authority that *"is* **not yet** *come"* is to continue for *"a* **short** *space."*

Look what happens when present world governments (iron and clay) are overcome by the **first beast: Scripture** says, *"...and power was given unto him to* **continue forty and two months"** (Revelation 13:5). The duration of the first beast is for **three and one-half years**—*"a short space."* The **first beast** is the **seventh** authority of earth. (The crowns move to the horns; in the future, there are ten rulers.) That fulfills the riddle for the identity of the seven kings (government by men).

God's Word has identified an authority of very **short** duration, **distinguishing** it from **all** other governments which lasted from lifetimes through hundreds of years. Historically, **no** other form of government has been as brief.

The first beast will not be overthrown; its rule is short

because after three and one-half years a **spiritual leader**, the **second** beast emerges, *"And he exerciseth all the **power** of the **first** beast before him..."* (Revelation 13:12). The first beast consisting of normal humans in authority (the beast with ten **horns** wearing crowns) will relinquish all of its authority to the second beast; the religious wonder, Antichrist. The second beast adds spiritual power to the world's physical government. The second beast does not destroy the first beast. He institutes an image symbolizing the first beast as an object of reverence (Revelation 13:12).

According to the above-listed Scriptures, the **second** beast (the **eighth** authority) receives physical government from the **first** beast (the **seventh** authority). *"And the **beast that was, and is not**, even **he is the eighth**, and **is of the seven**, and goeth into perdition"* (Revelation 17:11). That verse contains the identity for the eighth king. The **eighth** will **emerge** from one of the seven; it happens to be from the **seventh** authority. Satan (the dragon) **empowers** the seventh authority (the ten horns) which consists of normal humans (Revelation 13:2), and so he was considered *"of the seven."* The second beast, Antichrist, personifying Satan, is the **eighth** authority. That wicked government is directed by a devilish trinity. The eighth authority is the **same** as the beast from the first riddle, which *"was"* and *"is not"*—Satan.

That is how the second riddle returns and meshes with the first riddle. Satan personified, the one who *"shall ascend"* from Revelation 17:8, is **also** the **second** beast *"coming up out of the earth"* (Revelation 13:11). The second beast is the eighth government in the riddle concerning "seven kings."

Considering those Scriptures, this analysis reveals how Satan himself fulfills both riddles. He **returns** to greater **spiritual** authority and **also** becomes a **physical governing** authority on earth. That is what the riddles teach. At the conclusion, he will *"**go into perdition**"* (destruction); that corresponds in both riddles

(Revelation 17:8 and 11). According to Revelation 20:10, Satan ends up in the lake of fire—eternal destruction (perdition).

God has revealed in His Word what will occur; Scriptures blending together tell the story. Please **remember** that God makes divine provision for His overcoming church, even though Satan regains his title as *"prince of the power of the air."* Everyone **not** clinging to God **will** believe that Satan is God (2 Thessalonians 2:8-11).

THE SECOND BEAST

Revelation 17:8 says the beast *"shall ascend."* The following is a description of the **eighth** authority, the second beast from Revelation 13:11, 13-16:

> *"And I beheld another beast **coming up** (ascending) out of the earth; and he had two horns like a lamb, and he spake as a dragon...* [13] *And he doeth great wonders, so that he maketh fire come down from heaven on the earth in the sight of men, And deceiveth them that dwell on the earth by the means of those miracles which he had power to do in the sight of the beast; saying to them that dwell on the earth, that they should make an image to the beast, which had the wound by the sword, and did live. And he had power to give life unto the image of the beast, that the image of the beast should both speak, and cause that as many as would not worship the image of the beast should be killed. And he causeth all, both small and great, rich and poor, free and bond, to receive a mark in their right hand, or in their foreheads."*

Another relevant Scripture to be considered along with Revelation 13, is 2 Thessalonians 2:7-12:

> *"For the mystery of iniquity doth already work: only he who now letteth will let, until he be taken out of the way. **And then shall that Wicked be revealed**, whom the Lord shall consume with the spirit of his mouth, and shall destroy with the brightness of his coming: Even him, whose coming is after the working of **Satan with all power and signs and lying wonders**, And with all **deceivableness of***

146

unrighteousness in them that perish; because they received not the love of the truth, that they might be saved. And for this cause God shall send them strong delusion, that they should believe a lie: That they all might be damned who believed not the truth, but had pleasure in unrighteousness."

People who know God will not be deceived. Those people refusing to embrace the fullness of Christ and His authority are deceived and damned (v. 12).

According to Scripture, *"he who now letteth"* will be taken out of the way. To **allow** the eighth authority to rise, God withdraws some of the power and authority Jesus purchased at Calvary. In other words, Satan is **permitted** to receive authority again.

At certain times in history, huge spiritual changes occurred. Some of those times included the fall of Adam and Eve, God's covenant of circumcision with Abraham, the giving of the Law through Moses, and Jesus, the Initiator of the new covenant. Yet another spiritual change is on the way: *"until he be taken out of the way."* This passage teaches the Holy Spirit will be restrained from much spiritual influence over people; that enables Satan to rise into power again.

The following is **speculation** to ponder from the world of science fiction. A computer issuing governing instructions (laws) in the New World Order is also centrally in charge of finance and commerce. That computer is miraculously brought to life and given human attributes and mobility (an android, artificial intelligence). Satan takes credit for the miracle of "life." That miracle certainly fulfills the qualifications of a living, world-governing, financial authority. (The image that lived from Revelation 13:15.) Does that scenario have a potential of happening? At the very least, the possibility is thought-provoking.

In Revelation 13:11, the second beast only has **two horns**

147

(kings/authorities). Still, according to verse 12, it has the **same power** over mankind the first beast had with **ten horns** (the ten future kings). It is logical, the **two** horns are 1) **governmental/ financial** (ten horns from the first beast) and 2) **spiritual** authority (like the seven horns of the Lamb from Revelation 5:6). There are miracles: making fire come down from heaven (Revelation 13:13) and giving life to something that is inanimate (Revelation 13:15). God **allows** Antichrist to use the "spiritually miraculous" as an attempt to imitate Him (2 Thessalonians 2:11).

The first beast (**seventh** authority) will take the saints of God into captivity unless they physically fight him (Revelation 13:10). During the reign of the second beast (eighth authority), the Christian captives are martyred for refusing to worship the image of the beast and receive his mark, *"...and cause that as many as would not worship the image of the beast should be killed"* (Revelation 13:15). That theme is restated in Revelation 20:4, which says,

> *"And I saw thrones, and they sat upon them, and judgment was given unto them: and I saw the souls of them that were **beheaded for the witness of Jesus**, and for the word of God, and **which had not worshipped the beast, neither his image, neither had received his mark upon their foreheads or in their hands**; and they lived and reigned with Christ a thousand years."*

The second beast has the power of the first beast (governmental and financial); additionally, **spiritual** authority is given to it. The second beast has power to deceive everyone not embracing God's Truth (Revelation 13:14). This "dangerous thing" is referred to as "Antichrist." His is the number "666." Many through the ages have tried to predict his coming and identify his name. I have proposed the possible scenario for artificial

148

intelligence, an android to be involved. That is only a logical guess. There is no reason to guess about nationality, name, the actual year he rises, or anything else. **After** he rises into power and his position is established, his **number** will **verify** God's Truth concerning his identity.

There is **no coincidence** involved with the fulfillment of detailed prophecy. Two thousand years ago, the coming of Messiah was prophesied. The religious of the time, Pharisees, Sadducees, scribes, and priests, could **not predict** who Christ would be. **After** He arrived and **matched** the **prophecies**, Jesus was shown to be the fulfillment of God's Word. He was **proven** to be "the Christ" through **fulfillment** of **Scripture** and **miracles**.

The **same is true** of the coming Antichrist. The number of his name will confirm he was the one **prophesied**. It is not imperative for **today's** Christian to know who he is **before** he manifests. The overcomers (spiritually mature) will be under God's provision and protection from the first beast and Antichrist.

Two groups of **immature** Christians are not protected. The group willing to fight is killed for resisting the first beast when he overpowers current world governments (Revelation 13:7). The pacifists are taken captive; later, they are executed by the second beast, known as Antichrist (Revelation 13:15). They are primarily the ones needing to consider the "666," proving his identity.

It will be assuring for Christians in captivity to identify Antichrist by his number; they will not be deceived by miracles he performs. They need courage and faith to choose **spiritual life** over impending physical death by rejecting Antichrist and his mark. Knowing the number of his name (given from prophecy) will give them courage. It verifies God's Word. That is the crucial time period to know the number of Antichrist's name, his **positive identification number**; it is given by God for protection from deception and the **encouragement** of His people.

149

Pacifists living in captivity see the three personalities of Antichrist. The second beast has power and authority from Satan personified; he gives power to a false prophet, enabling him to do miracles (Revelation 13:13). The false prophet has an image (inanimate object) made that somehow represents a visual replica of the first beast (possibly an android). The image is brought to life, imitating the power of God to create life (Revelation 13:14, 15). That wicked trinity forms what is commonly identified as Antichrist (Revelation 20:10, 13:11). Within it, Satan personified, presents himself to be God, *"Who opposeth and **exalteth himself above all that is called God**, or that is worshipped; so that **he as God** sitteth in the temple of God, **showing himself that he is God"*** (2 Thessalonians 2:4).

Daniel had a vision of the **last** king—the second beast:

> *"And the king* [the beast] *shall do according to his will; and he shall **exalt himself**, and magnify **himself above** every god, and shall **speak marvelous things against the God of gods**, and shall prosper till the indignation be accomplished: for that that is determined shall be done"* (Daniel 11:36).

The deceptions of Antichrist are effectively convincing and even those under God's provision will be **tempted** to believe him. Jesus **warned** of that temptation in Matthew 24:24, *"For there shall arise false christs, and false prophets, and **shall show great signs and wonders**; insomuch that, **if** it were **possible**, they shall **deceive the very elect**."* While hidden for provision, the elect/overcomers can still be tempted. Revelation 3:11 says, *"Behold, I **come** quickly: **hold** that **fast** which thou **hast**, that no man **take** thy **crown*** [the overcomer's crown]."* The victory they won could be lost. That is what Jesus told the church of Philadelphia, a church protected from tribulation. It is possible for overcoming believers to fall away from the deliverance they receive. Knowing Antichrist's number will help them not to fall prey to deceptions.

Matthew 24:24 is the second time Jesus warns about **false** leaders. His first warning was early in the end-time events (Matthew 24:5). Those false leaders were addressed by the first seal. They did not perform miraculous signs and wonders; they "bent the truth." The false ones of Matthew 24:24 (late in the end-time events) will perform miracles; they are false prophets with power. **Deception** is a strong weapon for Satan.

According to Daniel 11:36, the king (Satan) will magnify himself above **every** god. That includes **all** of the different religions people follow. In the end-time, he is personified as the *"man of sin"* (2 Thessalonians 2:3, 4). Satan tries to copy the Holy Triune God in every way. He attempts a great deception, purposing to take more souls to hell with him; it is the only way that God can be hurt by him. **Be aware!** Learn to know and serve God Almighty—the Lord, Creator, Savior, King—and His Word; **you** will **not** be **deceived** when that time arrives!

The first and second beasts of Revelation are *"the prince that shall come,"* discovered in Daniel 9:26, 27. The first beast makes a covenant with Israel for "one week" (seven years); half-way, at three and one-half years, the second beast breaks the original covenant, declaring he is God.

The re-building of Israel's temple is a major portion of Israel's covenant with the beast; the street and the wall are built in "times of trouble" (Daniel 9:25).

Revelation is written for the church of Jesus Christ in which Messianic (saved) Jews are included. The intention of this writing is to focus on Jesus' church. Even though no obvious specifics in Revelation pertain to the Jews, Old Testament prophecies indicate that God deals with His people, Israel, when Jesus returns to initiate

151

the millennial reign. Remember what Jesus said about Israel:

> *"O Jerusalem, Jerusalem, thou that killest the prophets, and stonest them which are sent unto thee, how often would I have gathered thy children together, even as a hen gathereth her chickens under her wings, and ye would not! Behold, your* **house** *is left unto you* **desolate**. *For I say unto you,* **Ye shall not see me henceforth, till ye shall say, Blessed is he that cometh in the name of the Lord"** (Matthew 23:37-39).

Jesus' glorious return is the era He spoke of. Though Revelation is not written **for** Israel, Jesus has **not given up** on Israel.

WRATH AND THE RETURN OF CHRIST

After the **eighth** government (the second beast) is in authority and established, the trumpet and vial judgments (God's wrath) are cast upon the **wicked**. Overcoming believers are provided for and protected by God. The remaining believers (pacifists) have been martyred by the second beast—Antichrist. Those martyrs are with God in spirit and waiting for the first physical resurrection of the dead. After six wrath judgments are completed, the first resurrection happens instantly as Jesus returns (1 Thessalonians 4:16, Revelation 20:4, 5).

These are the days Jesus spoke of in Matthew 24:21, 22, as six of the seven wrath judgments are poured upon earth:

> *"For then shall be great tribulation, such as was not since the beginning of the world to this time, no, nor ever shall be. And except those days should be shortened, there should **no flesh** be saved: but for the **elect's sake** those days shall be **shortened**."*

The physical conditions of earth become so wretched from the wrath judgments, that if the days are not shortened, even the hidden overcomers would not survive.

Remember: the seventh seal (containing seven wrath judgments) is actually opened before the sixth seal (the return of Jesus). The return of Christ takes place at the **beginning** of the **seventh wrath** judgment—the final of seven judgments. Since overcomers are on earth through six of seven judgments, **the days will be shortened**.

Jesus ends the reign of Antichrist (the second beast) during His glorious return/rapture. God's Word describes Jesus' return in the following passages:

1 Thessalonians 4:14-17

"For if we believe that Jesus died and rose again, even so them also which sleep in Jesus will God bring with him. For this we say unto you by the word of the Lord, that we which are alive and remain unto the coming of the Lord shall not prevent them which are asleep. For the Lord himself shall descend from heaven with a shout, with the voice of the archangel, and with the trump of God: and the dead in Christ shall rise first: Then we which are alive and remain shall be caught up together with them in the clouds, to meet the Lord in the air: and so shall we ever be with the Lord."

Revelation 11:15-19

"And the seventh angel sounded; and there were great voices in heaven, saying, The kingdoms of this world are become the kingdoms of our Lord, and of his Christ; and he shall reign for ever and ever. And the four and twenty elders, which sat before God on their seats, fell upon their faces, and worshipped God, Saying, We give thee thanks, O Lord God Almighty, which art, and wast, and art to come; because thou hast taken to thee thy great power, and hast reigned. And the nations were angry, and thy wrath is come, and the time of the dead, that they should be judged, and that thou shouldest give reward unto thy servants the prophets, and to the saints, and them that fear thy name, small and great; and shouldest destroy them which destroy the earth. And the temple of God was opened in heaven, and there was seen in his temple the ark of his testament: and

*there were lightnings, and voices, and thunderings, and an
earthquake, and great hail."*

Revelation 16:17-21
   *"And the seventh angel poured out his vial into the
air; and there came a great voice out of the temple of
heaven, from the throne, saying, It is done. And there were
voices, and thunders, and lightnings; and there was a great
earthquake, such as was not since men were upon the earth,
so mighty an earthquake, and so great. And the great city
was divided into three parts, and the cities of the nations
fell: and great Babylon came in remembrance before God,
to give unto her the cup of the wine of the fierceness of his
wrath. And every island fled away, and the mountains were
not found. And there fell upon men a great hail out of
heaven, every stone about the weight of a talent: and men
blasphemed God because of the plague of the hail; for the
plague thereof was exceeding great."*

Matthew 24:29-31
   *"Immediately after the tribulation of those days
shall the sun be darkened, and the moon shall not give her
light, and the stars shall fall from heaven, and the powers of
the heavens shall be shaken: And then shall appear the sign
of the Son of man in heaven: and then shall all the tribes of
the earth mourn, and they shall see the Son of man coming
in the clouds of heaven with power and great glory. And he
shall send his angels with a great sound of a trumpet, and
they shall gather together his elect from the four winds, from
one end of heaven to the other."*

Revelation 6:12-17

*"And I beheld when he had opened the sixth seal,
and, lo, there was a great earthquake; and the sun became
black as sackcloth of hair, and the moon became as blood;
And the stars of heaven fell unto the earth, even as a fig tree
casteth her untimely figs, when she is shaken of a mighty
wind. And the heaven departed as a scroll when it is rolled
together; and every mountain and island were moved out of
their places. And the kings of the earth, and the great men,
and the rich men, and the chief captains, and the mighty
men, and every bondman, and every free man, hid
themselves in the dens and in the rocks of the mountains;
And said to the mountains and rocks, Fall on us, and hide us
from the face of him that sitteth on the throne, and from the
wrath of the Lamb: For the great day of his wrath is come;
and who shall be able to stand?"*

Revelation 19:11-16

*"And I saw heaven opened, and behold a white
horse; and he that sat upon him was called Faithful and
True, and in righteousness he doth judge and make war. His
eyes were as a flame of fire, and on his head were many
crowns; and he had a name written, that no man knew, but
he himself. And he was clothed with a vesture dipped in
blood: and his name is called The Word of God. And the
armies which were in heaven followed him upon white
horses, clothed in fine linen, white and clean. And out of his
mouth goeth a sharp sword, that with it he should smite the
nations: and he shall rule them with a rod of iron: and he
treadeth the winepress of the fierceness and wrath of
Almighty God. And he hath on his vesture and on his thigh a
name written, KING OF KINGS, AND LORD OF LORDS."*

Jesus returns to tread the **winepress** of the **wrath of God** (Revelation 19:15); that is distinctly different from the seven wrath judgments dispensed by angels.

Jesus returns with the anger of God; Antichrist and the wicked will wage war against Jesus and His servants. This time **Jesus' Word** destroys His enemies. At the **end** of His one-thousand-year reign, something different is observed.

His Word (the sword from His mouth) is His **command** to **His armies** to go into battle as He returns. The phenomena of this passage match previous Scriptures describing His return. By resurrection and rapture of physical bodies, Jesus' servants are with Him. They now have supernatural bodies.

*"Blow ye the trumpet in Zion and sound an alarm in my holy mountain: let all the inhabitants of the land tremble: **for the day of the LORD cometh**, for it is nigh at hand; A day of darkness and of gloominess, a day of clouds and of thick darkness, as the morning spread upon the mountains: a great people and a strong; there hath not been ever the like, neither shall be any more after it, even to the years of many generations. A fire devoureth before them; and behind them a flame burneth: the land is as the garden of Eden before them, and behind them a desolate wilderness; yea, and nothing shall escape them. The appearance of them is as the appearance of horses; and as horsemen, so shall they run. Like the noise of chariots on the tops of mountains shall they leap, like the noise of a flame of fire that devoureth the stubble, as a strong people set in battle array. Before their face the people shall be much pained: all faces shall gather blackness. They shall run like mighty men; they shall climb the wall like men of war; and they shall march everyone on*

*his ways, and they shall not break their ranks: Neither shall one thrust another; they shall walk everyone in his path: and **when they fall upon the sword, they shall not be wounded**. They shall run to and fro in the city; they shall run upon the wall, they shall climb up upon the houses; they shall enter in at the windows like a thief. The **earth shall quake** before them; the **heavens shall tremble**: the **sun and the moon shall be dark**, and the **stars shall withdraw** their **shining**: And the **LORD shall utter His voice** before his army: for his camp is very great: for he is strong that executeth his word: for **the day of the LORD** is great and very terrible; and who can abide it"* (Joel 2:1-11)?

If someone from the Lord's army were to be struck with a sword (weapon), they will not be wounded. All of the Lord's armies will be in glorified bodies, products of resurrection and rapture. Those bodies will be similar in nature to Christ's body after His resurrection from the dead.

*"Then the same day at evening, being the first day of the week, **when the doors were shut** where the disciples were assembled for fear of the Jews, **came Jesus and stood** in the midst, and saith unto them, Peace be unto you"* (John 20:19).

He came into a locked room and no one opened the door.

*"And when he had spoken these things, while they beheld, **he was taken up**; and a cloud received him out of their sight. And while they looked steadfastly **toward heaven as he went up**, behold, two men stood by them in white apparel; Which also said, Ye men of Galilee, why stand ye*

158

*gazing up into heaven? this same Jesus, which is taken up from you into heaven, **shall so come in like manner** as ye have seen him go into heaven"* (Acts 1:9-11).

Doors, walls, and gravity do not have any effect on glorified bodies. The prophecy from Joel indicates the mere weapons of mankind have no effect on the armies of Jesus. Joel 2:10 states the earth will quake before them, the heavens tremble, the sun, moon and stars will be dark. Please reread the sixth seal in Revelation 6:12, 13. The **same** event is described by both passages.

According to Matthew 24:31, the elect are gathered *"...from the four winds, from one end of heaven to the other."* Remember John's location as he watched four angels holding the four winds of earth in Revelation 7:1-3? Other angels sealed the servants of God. The place that sealing occurred (the four winds) is the **same** place from which angels **gather** the **elect** (Matthew 24:31).

God will likely provide multiple places of hiding and provision for twelve groups of His elect. When Jesus reveals Himself for provision, it will be by Spirit, i.e., being multiple places simultaneously. By Spirit, Jesus is not limited to be one place at a time. God is omnipresent and cares for all of His people. The diagram of the twelve tribes around the tabernacle (sealing of 144,000) perfectly describes the location for gathering the elect by God's angels.

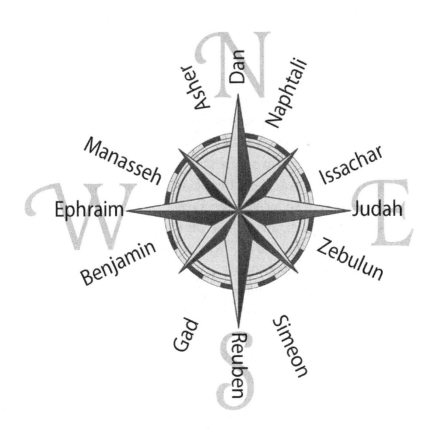

THE MILLENNIAL REIGN

The glorious return of Christ begins what is referred to as the millennial reign. In supreme authority, Jesus governs the entire earth for 1,000 years and his servants rule and reign with Him (Revelation 20:6). This refers to the **physical** kingdom of God—not the spiritual (forthcoming study).

Two personalities of the wicked trinity/second beast/Antichrist are cast into the lake of fire, their permanent end (Revelation 19:20). These (the living image and false prophet) are the two horns (government and religion) that were on the wicked lamb. They represent **physical** rule through **governments** and **finances** (the image of the first beast brought to life) and the **spiritual** rule (religion) of the false prophet (Revelation 13:11). There is one prominent world government and religion under Antichrist, but that does not mean there is world peace and unity. On the contrary, it instead means that Antichrist **subdues** all **organized** government and religion while conflicts continue.

An angel from God chains and binds Satan (the third part of the wicked trinity, the wicked lamb) for 1,000 years so that he **cannot deceive anyone** for that time period (Revelation 20:2, 3).

* * * * *

Revelation chapter ten mentions a concealed mystery. John observes a powerful angel holding a book in his hand; the angel speaks with a lion's roar and then seven thunders uttered. John was **forbidden** to write what the thunders said. After they uttered, the angel declared that **time** would cease (Revelation 10:1-6).

That is a very noteworthy occurrence. While hidden from unfaithful people, God is letting observant believers know how long it takes to bring all of His purposes for this world to completion. The creation of the heavens marked the beginning of time; *seasons, days* and *years* began at creation in Genesis 1:14, when God created the sun, moon, and stars (vv. 15-18). After the thunders finished speaking, the angel said, *"...there should be **time** no longer"* (Revelation 10:6). Time, as presently understood, will cease. Time began at creation in Genesis; it ends in Revelation. In Revelation 21:1, heaven and earth (creation) **pass away** and are **replaced** by *"a new heaven and a new earth."* (Also see Isaiah 65:17.) In the new creation, the glory of God is the light and there is **no darkness** (Revelation 22:5); time cannot be measured by seasons, days and years; it will cease when the **new** creation begins.

Approximately 2,000 years elapsed from Adam to Abraham; there was no covenant from God, and men did what was right in their own sight. Approximately 2,000 years passed from Abraham to Jesus; God gave Old Testament Law for relationship with Him. It identified sin. Approximately 2,000 years lapsed from Jesus to the present, the Church Age, an era when the Holy Spirit brings the "living law" inside of every believer; however, Satan is still deceiving mankind. During the millennial reign, Jesus will bring perfect government and relationship with God to the earth for 1,000 years. Satan is bound and unable to deceive anyone.

Approximately 6,000 years have elapsed **prior** to Jesus' millennial reign. The probability that God will fulfill Revelation's doubled prophecies in the near future is very real. Time is up; **it is soon time** for the millennial reign of Jesus. **Each individual thunder** must have pronounced "1,000 years." "Seven" is known as God's number of completion. Each one of the seven thunders uttering "1000 years" is in perfect agreement (7 x 1000 = 7000). Then world history is concluded; there is termination of the currently known heaven and earth, and time ceases to exist.

With God one day is as a thousand years, and a thousand years as one day (2 Peter 3:8). The glory of God gives light; there is no darkness with Him to mark the passage of time. Creation measures time according to the seasons, days and years of creation. God's creation does not affect Him or change His perspective on anything. He is the same as He has always been and eternally will be; it is creation that ages and changes. Obviously, much of what humans call knowledge and science is foolishness when it deviates from God's Word (1 Corinthians 1:25).

The millennial reign of Jesus (the seventh day) is a "day of rest" for the world. For six days mankind has brought wickedness into the world; on the seventh day, Jesus brings peace and righteousness.

It is puzzling to comprehend why humankind would ever want to fight against Jesus after He has **justly** ruled them. Scripture declares that after 1,000 years, Satan will be loosed and will again **deceive** the people.

According to Revelation 20:7-9, Satan *"...shall go out to deceive the nations...."* He will **again use** the powerful weapon of DECEPTION enticing people to rebel against Jesus. There will be a war. Many people will rise up against Jesus and His servants (those of the first resurrection). Jesus and those ruling with Him will be surrounded by Satan and the many people he has **deceived**. Deception is the same weapon he used on Eve and all of mankind for 6,000 years.

Deception is accomplished by influencing people to **doubt** that God and His Word are true. If people doubt God's Truth, they can be **tempted** to compromise living as He commanded. Once they **compromise** their behavior, they **break** the commands and laws of God. When they break His commands and laws, they do **not** love God with all of their heart, mind, soul, and strength (the **first** and **greatest** commandment). When humans don't love God, Satan has a very good chance of **snaring** additional souls from the pathway of life, to place them on the highway to hell; it's the **only** way he can hurt God.

Promoting doubt of God and His Word to produce compromise is effective; that weapon was proven successful by standing the test of time. In the beginning, it worked on Eve, it was the counsel of Balaam to corrupt Israel, and is currently a plague to Jesus' church. In the future, Satan will use it one last time to lure people into a war against Jesus. Watch out for **deception**; it produces **doubt** that results in the **compromise** of Truth, which then leads to **disobedience**. Protect yourself; believe and live all of God's Truth without doubting one word.

Deception works subtly and sometimes over long periods of time. All it takes is one willing human mind for Satan to start the process. Utilizing the topic of evolution, the method Satan initiates can be readily observed.

Satan's first move is to affect a person's **thoughts**. Charles Darwin was sent to the liberal Edinburg University by his physician father. After he was exposed to "freethinkers" renouncing divine design (creation), his dad was concerned and sent him to Christ's College at Cambridge, a conservative college by comparison. (Christ's College rejected "freethinkers.") Though he was sent there, Charles' friend Robert Grant promoted evolution to Darwin. Through education, thoughts were placed into Darwin's mind. He **pondered** the subject instead of instantly **dismissing** the **thoughts**. The process of **deception** was **initiated**; it led to **doubt** that God had created all things. The freethinkers introduced those thoughts to him and encouraged him to begin a **reasoning** process. Darwin **rationalized** that some species of animals were similar and one **might** have changed into the other over extended periods of time. That is the first step of Satan's deception, doubt of God's Word and subjecting It to human intellect. (A place Satan can gain influence.)

At that point, Darwin fully received the **deception**, an **alternative** to the **truth** of creation. God's Word calls it *"...oppositions of science falsely so called"* (1 Timothy 6:20). Once

164

the **doubt** of one **truth** took root, the **compromise** of **other truths** began. If there was no personal involvement by God in creation, He is simply some force that is out in space somewhere. Thus, a woman should have the right to terminate a baby in her womb. She reasons that it is her body and she has the right to do so. The theory introduced to the world through Darwin compromised God's Truth and enticed a woman to disobey His commandment, *"Thou shalt not kill."* She was deceived by Satan and the one he enticed to develop the theory. Abortion became acceptable because Satan's deception originated from an intelligent human. The **origin** of Darwin's thoughts (the denial of creation) was from Satan. Years later, it was difficult for the woman to comprehend the origin of what she was taught, so she was **deceived** into error. She was caught by the same trap that snared Eve; the snare was planted by analytic thoughts developed while forsaking God's Word. She **reasoned** it was her body; God was taken out of consideration when she was deceived, believing Darwin's theory. Her intellectual reasoning determined right from wrong. In effect, she perceived she had wisdom as though she were God. Satan continues using that ploy today.

That scenario illustrates how deception within human thoughts introduces doubt. Doubt fosters the compromise of truth and ends up as sin. Satan **initiates thoughts** to manufacture doubt and to challenge every attribute in the Word of God. It is a powerfully effective weapon against mankind's faith in God.

In their own eyes, humans see themselves as being intelligent, not realizing that Satan can affect the intellect. It is one of his primary targets. That is why colleges (other than conservative Christian) foster so much liberal thinking. Academically advanced humans see nothing wrong with opposing God's Word; thereby, as Darwin, they become deceived by Satan in many viewpoints. The advancements civilization has received through academic progressions are counterbalanced by losses to faith and moral fiber in those receiving education. After years of studying and thousands of dollars spent, they have humanism for a god and no understanding concerning the Truth of the Living God; most secular schooling increasingly ridicules faith instead of supporting it.

Through fallen nature, humans wish to reason for themselves **instead of simply obeying God**; Satan finds fertile grounds to plant seeds of deceit. Satan's deception got Eve into trouble; the **desire** for **wisdom** (her intellect), enticed her to disobey God, *"...and a tree to be **desired** to make one **wise**..."* (Genesis 3:6). Humans are still falling for the **same** deception from Satan; they desire wisdom and to determine right from wrong for themselves, i.e., to *"...be as gods, knowing good and evil"* (v. 5).

The last time Satan uses deception on people is at the end of the millennial reign. From the beginning to end, doubting God bears catastrophic consequences. Don't allow any portion of His Word to be attacked or explained as invalid. Satan knows what God said; he tried to tempt Jesus by **twisting** the truth; he will try the **same tactics** with you. Reject the first thought that disagrees with any portion of Scripture; **don't entertain it**. Pondering will only lead toward doubting God. If you don't know what God said, prioritize learning. More important than anything else is learning what He said (Matthew 6:33). If time is not set aside to learn, a person doesn't really care where his or her soul spends eternity.

Satan's war against Jesus is the last confrontation to be fought on earth. This final battle is also the **final** act of Satan; he will be judged and punished **forever** (Revelation 20:7-10). It won't be much of a battle, as verse 9 states, *"...fire came down from God out of heaven, and devoured them."* This time, God the Father will destroy all of the people joining with Satan to war against His Son. That battle is the finale of the millennial reign.

THE WHITE THRONE JUDGMENT

The millennial reign is followed by the Great White Throne Judgment. There is a distinction between the Great White Throne Judgment and the judgment seat of Christ. Those believers previously proving their faith and obedience to God were part of the first resurrection or rapture and will **not be part** of the Great White Throne Judgment. They were already resurrected and have ruled and reigned with Christ (Revelation 20:4-6). They built their foundation on Jesus and their works were tested and approved by fire (1 Corinthians 3:11-15). Those have stood before the judgment seat of Christ (Romans 14:10).

The Great White Throne Judgment is for all the remaining souls of mankind from both BC and AD. Those souls must now stand before God.

"And I saw a great white throne, and him that sat on it, from whose face the earth and the heaven fled away; and there was found no place for them. And I saw the dead, small and great, stand before God; and the books were opened: and another book was opened, which is the book of life: and the dead were judged out of those things which were written in the books, according to their works. And the sea gave up the dead which were in it; and death and hell delivered up the dead which were in them: and they were judged every man according to their works. And death and hell were cast into the lake of fire. This is the second death. And whosoever was not found written in the book of life was cast into the lake of fire" (Revelation 20:11-15).

A passage in the book of Daniel describes this event from a

Jewish perspective.

> *"And at that time shall Michael stand up, the great prince which standeth for the children of thy people: and there shall be a time of trouble, such as never was since there was a nation even to that same time: and at that time thy people shall be delivered, everyone that shall be found **written in the book**. And many of them that sleep in the dust of the earth **shall awake**, some to **everlasting life**, and some to shame and **everlasting contempt**"* (Daniel 12:1, 2).

In The White Throne Judgment, souls found written in God's Book of Life are raised from death. By speculation, they should mostly be Old Testament people such as Daniel, *"But go thou thy way **till the end be**: for thou shalt rest, and **stand** in thy lot at the **end** of the days"* (Daniel 12:13). Moses also knew that such a book existed (Exodus 32:31-33).

Possibly, people have existed in remote parts of earth who have never heard the Truth of God. They will be judged according to Romans 2:11-16:

> *"For there is no respect of persons with God. For as many as have sinned without law shall also perish without law: and as many as have sinned in the law shall be judged by the law; (For not the hearers of the law are just before God, but the doers of the law shall be justified. For when the Gentiles, which have not the law, do by nature the things contained in the law, these, having not the law, are a law unto themselves: Which show the work of the law written in their hearts, their conscience also bearing witness, and their thoughts the mean while accusing or else excusing one another;) **In the day when God shall judge the secrets of***

men by Jesus Christ according to my gospel."

It is not the place of humans to completely understand God's just judgments. **He is perfectly just**, and that knowledge is sufficient.

New heaven and a new earth are created after the Great White Throne Judgment. The first heaven and first earth pass away (Revelation 21:1), and *"...there should be **time** no longer"* (Revelation 10:6). The New Jerusalem, a place of great beauty and abundance is the dwelling place where God and His people will always be together. I encourage everyone to read Revelation 21. Explaining that chapter with words other than those already written would be difficult.

Revelation 22 continues to describe the beauty of New Jerusalem. Verse 7 says that believers are **blessed** to keep the prophecy of this book. God wants every believer to know, that living life with the knowledge of Revelation has a wonderful impact on him; every believer is **blessed**. Studying Revelation brings knowledge of what the future holds. Revelation is the **only** biblical book elaborating the **blessing** given to the **reader** and those who **hear**.

CLOSING THOUGHTS FOR REVELATION

This writing presented a distinctive view and interpretation of Revelation. Most of it interlinked Scripture with Scripture to reveal interpretation, rather than expounding ideas based on human understanding or history. For that reason, many scriptural quotes needed to be contained in it. Interpretation is given through God's Word—**Scripture explaining Scripture**.

Understanding what Revelation teaches can bring solemnity. Remember though, **God** called the ones receiving the knowledge of this book *"blessed."*

Spiritual maturity is the "fruit" produced in those giving God authority in their lives. The end result of maturity is to be miraculously **hidden** and **provided** for during the end-time. Those refusing to give God **all authority** now, but endure trials later, can choose eternal life. It is at the cost of martyrdom.

How are spiritual growth and the resulting blessedness possible? They are possible through grace: "divine influence upon the heart and its reflection in the life." **God honors the prayer** of those asking Him to work in them. If believers cooperate, the work is accomplished through His Holy Spirit and power.

God knew no one would fulfill the law, so He sent His Son and then His Spirit. Now He expects believers to walk in His ways and become overcomers by His Spirit. Christians are given an example of this through Paul: *"And herein do I exercise myself, to have always a conscience void of offense toward God, and toward men"* (Acts 24:16).

Living with an undefiled conscience leads believers to live the new covenant of God. He puts His laws inside and then empowers them by His Spirit. The Holy Spirit teaches, reigns and lives within Christians. Early church leaders were careful to have a clean conscience (Hebrews 13:18). Some end-time leaders will have a *conscience seared with a hot iron*, as they depart from the true faith (1 Timothy 4:1, 2).

The next section of this book elaborates on how God operates **in** faithful people.

SECTION TWO

Because of Revelation, two verses of Scripture rise from obscurity clearly informing Christians how to prepare for the end-time. These passages were introduced at the beginning of this book.

Zephaniah 2:3
> *"Seek ye the LORD, all ye meek of the earth, which have wrought his judgment; seek righteousness, seek meekness: it may be ye shall be hid in the day of the LORD's anger."*

Luke 21:36
> *"Watch ye therefore, and pray always, that ye may be accounted worthy to escape all these things that shall come to pass, and to stand before the Son of Man."*

Ponder what is coming **in** Revelation; the above passages have gained significantly more meaning. Zephaniah instructs people to seek righteousness and meekness—**after** they *"wrought his judgment."* After living by God's behavioral standards, the believer is **still** to be **seeking** righteousness and meekness. The result is that *"...it may be ye shall be **hid** in the day of the LORD's anger."* Everyone should be aware of the reward Scripture decrees. The potential for God's divine protection is provided: *"...**it may be ye shall be hid in the day** of the LORD's anger";* being hidden is optional. A person has to qualify to receive. Believers are directed to seek meekness and righteousness in order to receive the reward.

In Luke 21:36, the first command Jesus mentions is to

"watch," meaning "to keep awake." In other words, "stay alert." Jesus revealed all matters leading into the end-time and His return. Then He commanded, *"**Watch**."* He spoke in a tense portraying repeated action—not just once and done, but keep watching.

The second instruction is to *"**pray always**."* The word for *pray* in Greek is "a petition," from a root word meaning "to beg." *"Pray always"* is not a light prayer uttered frivolously; rather, it is an earnest petition given in a continuous sense. Jesus taught believers to zealously *"pray **always**...to **escape**."*

Jesus is talking to disciples (believers). They are to be praying to escape. His focus is not directed at the unsaved, but **believers**. Revelation reveals more than **one** category for believers. That is why this prayer becomes significant. Anyone desiring to escape martyrdom needs to take it seriously. Revelation discloses **why** believers need to pray. Revelation exposes the things believers will want to escape from.

This section explores **how** God works to mold and shape faithful servants to become mature. His Word teaches **how** to **escape** great tribulation.

The Holy Spirit

The Holy Spirit is a part of the Triune Godhead and Christian faith. Unfortunately, He is very often overlooked or neglected. A careful examination of God's Word reveals many aspects about Him that are not emphasized in many churches.

Consider prophecy concerning God's Spirit: Ezekiel 36:27 says, *"And I will put my spirit within you, and cause you to walk in my statutes, and ye shall keep my judgments, and do them."* Hundreds of years before Christ, God said through the prophet Ezekiel, He would put His Spirit **within** His people. Then, His Spirit initiates alteration in behavior within the believer. The Spirit of God *within* has impact; people walk in **His** statutes and keep **His** judgments. His Spirit within the believer is the *cause* of transformation. That was a radical thought at approximately 590 BC.

His Spirit would "come upon" people during the Old Testament. The difference in the New Testament is recorded by I Corinthians 6:19, which says, *"What? know ye not that your body is the temple of the Holy Ghost which is in you, which ye have of God, and ye are not your own?"* The Holy Spirit has authority and resides **within** human beings. Christians do **not have authority** over their lives. They have been purchased by Christ *"...ye are not your own."* Jesus is Lord (Master); the body of a believer is the dwelling place (temple) of God. That is further verified in Romans 8:9, 14:

> *"But ye are not in the flesh, but in the Spirit, if so be that the Spirit of God **dwell in you**. Now if any man **have not** the **Spirit** of Christ, he is **none** of his...[14]For as many as are **led** by the **Spirit** of God, **they** are the **sons** of God."*

174

The Holy Spirit dwells within and is the determining factor as to whether or not someone is Christian!

The Holy Spirit is **confirmation** to Christians that they are **bought** by Christ.

> *"In whom ye also trusted, after that ye heard the word of* ***truth,*** *the* ***gospel*** *of your* ***salvation:*** *in whom also* ***after that*** ***ye believed,*** *ye were* ***sealed*** *with that* ***Holy Spirit*** *of* ***promise,*** *Which is the* ***earnest*** *of our* ***inheritance*** *until the* ***redemption*** *of the* ***purchased possession,*** *unto the praise of his glory"* (Ephesians 1:13, 14).

The Greek definition for *earnest* is: "a pledge, i.e., a **part** of the purchase money or property **given in advance** as security for the rest." The Holy Spirit dwells within; **He** is the **advance** deposit, the security assuring the coming complete redemption. **Christians** are the *"purchased possession"* to be **redeemed** by **God**. What tremendous reassurance! The presence of the **Holy Spirit confirms** a **Christian** belongs to God. God gives a thirty-three and one-third percent down payment as security. His Spirit is real and His presence discernable; believers know without doubt, Christianity is the one true faith of all religions in this world. The *down payment* lives within them!

Peter said the Holy Ghost is given to those who obey God (Acts 5:32). It would be prudent for every believer to be bold enough to ask God for assurance His Spirit is indwelling them. God gives assurance in the way He chooses. He may manifest a spiritual gift or reveal dynamic behavioral changes occurring only because of His influence. Those changes are listed in Galatians 5:22-24. **If** His Spirit is in a believer, that person is changing. The Holy Spirit is reshaping every believer to become the image of Christ.

2 Timothy 1:14 tells us, *"That good thing which was*

committed unto thee **keep** *by the Holy Ghost which* **dwelleth in us.**"
He resides within; this verse expresses He has **power** to *keep* the
faithful. Jesus **kept** His disciples so that none were lost except the
"*son of perdition*," Judas (John 17:12). Faith is **sustained** by the
power of God.

Power...when believers are conscious of the Holy Spirit, He
brings power into their lives (Acts 1:8). When Jesus came to earth
as a baby, He laid down **all** His authority, position, and power in
order to become human. When the Holy Spirit came, He never laid
down **any** of His authority, position, or power. He came as
Almighty God. He enters the inner being of all believers with **all**
His authority, position, and power!

How is it possible for God to live within a Christian? Look
at what Jesus said to His disciples **before** the **atonement** of the
cross:

> "*If ye love me, keep my commandments. And I will pray the
> Father, and he shall give you another Comforter, that he
> may* **abide with you forever***; Even the* **Spirit of truth***; whom
> the world cannot receive, because it seeth him not, neither
> knoweth him: but ye know him;* **for he** dwelleth with you,
> **and** shall be in you*" (John 14:15-17).

He was **with** them, and He "***shall be in you.***" After the crucifixion's
atonement, believers were washed and could receive God's Spirit
inside of their bodies. The prophecy from Ezekiel 36:27 was
fulfilled because of Christ, but it could not happen until **after** He
made atonement for sin. The cleansing from sin through Christ
produced thorough purification enabling God to **dwell inside**
humans.

During His human lifetime, Jesus was "*Immanuel,*"
meaning "God **with** us;" God dwelling on earth as a man with

176

mankind. After the cross, the Holy Spirit was implanted within believers. Christians are **infused** with the power and authority of God; the Holy Spirit is "God **in** us."

A look at Scripture helps grasp how the Holy Spirit affects a believer. The more aware of Him a believer becomes, the more sensitized he is to His voice. In the conscience, the Spirit will guide, direct, correct, approve or disapprove of every unction, action, thought or word expressed.

He brings remembrance for Scripture. He grows spiritual fruits and gives spiritual gifts. *"For as many as are **led** by the Spirit of God, they are the sons of God"* (Romans 8:14). When someone deems he knows the direction of the Spirit, he is to **obey**.

Consider the following Scriptures: John 14:26, *"But the Comforter, which is the Holy Ghost, whom the Father will send in my name, **he shall teach** you all things, and **bring all things** to your remembrance, whatsoever I have said unto you."* He teaches and enables Christians to remember His Word. He enlightens Scripture verses; He teaches correct doctrine:

> 1 Corinthians 2:12-14, *"Now we have received, not the spirit of the world, but the **spirit** which is of **God**; **that we might know** the things that are freely **given** to **us of God**. Which things also we speak, **not** in the words which **man's wisdom** teaches, but which the **Holy Ghost teacheth**; comparing **spiritual** things with **spiritual**. But the natural man **receiveth not** the things of the Spirit of God: for they are **foolishness** unto him: neither can he know them, because they are **spiritually discerned**."*

He does **not** teach multiple interpretations of Scripture; He only teaches truth. Unsaved intellectuals cannot comprehend it. They are *"...ever learning, and **never able** to come to the knowledge of the* *truth"* (2 Timothy 3:7).

Ephesians 1:17 says, *"That the God of our Lord Jesus Christ, the Father of Glory, may give unto you the spirit of wisdom and revelation in the knowledge of him."* God reveals *"knowledge"* of Himself, what He is like; it is received via spirit.

In 1 Peter 1:22 we find, *"Seeing you have purified your souls in obeying the truth through the Spirit...."* He is the **power** of God to **obey** truth. Believers cooperate with Him as He leads them. They cannot successfully change behavior through only their own discipline. Trying to do so will lead to failure. Believers are purified *"through the Spirit."* Obedience to Him and trust in His power produces the change.

> *"Endeavoring to keep the **unity of the Spirit** in the bond of peace. There is **one body**, and **one Spirit**, even as ye are called in one hope of your calling"* (Ephesians 4:3, 4).

The Holy Spirit brings unity into the body of Christ. Christians must endeavor to follow Him as **He leads** them into unity. The body of Christ needs to realize, God's **goal** is to unify them. Everyone, all parts of the "body" are supposed to function as a single unit—"one." Unity can only be realized if all individuals obey the leading of the Spirit. A unified body begins with you and me—individuals obedient to the Spirit and Word of God.

1 Corinthians 12:7 says, *"But the **manifestation** [literally: exhibition] of the Spirit is given to **every** man to profit withal."* **Every** believer will display some gift or gifts of **power** during his lifetime. If the Holy Spirit is dwelling inside, at some point He will reveal Himself through exhibited power, unless He is quenched... extinguished. Verses **7 and 11** say, *"every man;"* no one is neglected.

Some churches say the dispensation for spiritual gifts ended

178

when the Bible was canonized; that which is "perfect" came to exist (1 Corinthians 13:8-10). If that were true and "perfection" has arrived, from which manuscripts should the churches read, and why are there so many different denominations and theological disagreements among believers? Additionally, a cliché declares that "you don't really know someone until you live with them." According to the description for the time of "perfection," people will deeply comprehend one another (v. 12). Human relationships have yet to change so that people excel at knowing one another. Perfection **cannot** be here yet. It will arrive with the millennial reign of Jesus, the end of the Church Age. His presence will end the need for the *prophecies, tongues,* and *knowledge* that pass away when perfection arrives (v. 8). Until He comes, believers still need *prophecies* to *edify* (literally: build up); individuals still need *edified* in their souls (*tongues* [1Corinthians 14:4]); Christians still need growth in the *knowledge* of God. During the millennial reign, Jesus is physically with mankind again; the need for spiritual gifting ends when He returns. The millennial reign is *"when that which is perfect is come,"* not the biblical canonization.

Churches may contend by saying manifestation power gifts stopped after the first century. Pentecostalism emerged and tried to revive them in the early 1900s. A dynamic move of God took place at that time, but throughout the church era, some people have been sensitive to the spiritual realm. They were not labeled Pentecostal, but rather as "mystics." St. Francis of Assisi was among the most notable. Gifts of power are found in believers after the first century. (Note: St. Francis lived more than three centuries before the Reformation; he is a common predecessor for today's Protestant and Catholic Churches.)

Some churches say the gifts died with the apostles. That assumption is impossible; the Holy Spirit gave gifts to the apostles and other believers as He dwelled inside of them. The Holy Spirit

lived inside the apostles precisely as He **lives inside** Christians
today. The **age** for the **Holy Spirit** to **dwell within** believers did
not end. In fact, if He is not in a person, that person is **not saved**
(Romans 8:9). The Holy Spirit did **not change** or **lose** any of **His
power** through the years. Present-day Christians and the apostles
receive the **same power source**. The Christian's **body** is a **vessel**
God uses to **exhibit His power** by His Spirit.

Whether a person drives an antique sports car or a modern
one does not matter. He is still the same driver with the same skills;
the only change has been the vehicle. The Holy Spirit is within
modern-day Christians, and He was within their predecessors.
Obey Scripture: never stop the Holy Spirit. Don't teach **against**
Him exhibiting gifts of power in believers.

When Jesus was on earth, many people followed Him
wherever He went. They wanted to **experience all** He did and said.
Now the Holy Spirit is with the church; there are those not wanting
to experience what He does or says; something's wrong.

"Quench not the Spirit. Despise not prophesyings" (1
Thessalonians 5:19, 20).

1 Corinthians 12:7 and 11 say **everyone** will manifest one or
more gifts. Those Scriptures were **never** biblically nullified.

Some Christians may feel "Spirit-filled, full gospel"
churches are promoted through this manner of explaining the Holy
Spirit. Biblical **accuracy** is of **foremost** importance for this writing.
If an end to gifts is not recorded by Scripture, no one should teach
they have ended, or **evade** them by adhering to the reasoning of
men. Biblically described spiritual relationship with God is being
presented. An additional Christian label for that is unnecessary. The
Holy Spirit along with His power are to be **promoted** and **sought
after—not abandoned** or **ignored**.

In review, the Holy Spirit lives in believers, directs their lives, teaches truth, quickens memory for Scripture, gives wisdom and revelation of God, provides power to obey truth, grants spiritual gifts for service with power, and unifies the body of Christ.

Consider the above-listed activities of the Holy Spirit. Satan achieved one of his greatest victories against the church when he enticed believers to accept an academically focused relationship with God. Instead of seeking the Spirit for power and direction in faith, the study of God and His Word became an intellectual pursuit. **Focus** was drawn away from the Spirit—the One Who leads every believer and the church. Academic theology **acknowledges** the presence of the Holy Spirit, but does **not** seek **any tangible** power **because** of His existence. He is simply understood to exist. It does not **stress** His activity as outlined in the previous paragraph.

Satan struck at the **power source** for the church. Weakening the power of the Spirit's influence via human desire to learn for themselves through academics, Satan could begin twisting God's Word via human intellect; that is what happened with Eve. Instead of every Scripture being incorporated into doctrine, a select few could be used by applying human reasoning and knowledge through scholarship. Any Scripture offering a different conclusion than the one desired is explained away by deduction, or is simply ignored. Satan's tactic was successful; proof is realized by the weakness in much of today's church in comparison to the biblical description of the early church.

Churches need to repent; **restoring desire** for the Spirit is the beginning. Jesus cultivated anticipation in His disciples, calling the Comforter the *"promise"* from the Father. The Father's promise is to be **sought** after. They were instructed to wait for it in Jerusalem, but He didn't tell them how long. He said to wait **until** they were *"...endued with power from on high"* (Luke 24:49). That awaiting is the necessary attitude, and they waited in expectation.

181

After the Holy Spirit comes in power, believers follow Him. They do not tell Him to follow them; the Spirit leads as He pleases without restrictions, inside the church or individuals. When He is in control, He will **not** be told to move as He wants for a 20 minute sermon and then stop so church can be dismissed. That is a place academics have led the church into, not the Holy Spirit.

Attitude for Holy Spirit-led service to God is observed in the nature of the prayers believers speak. Seeking to please God by following His Spirit transforms human attitude. When beseeching God, Spirit-led believers should say, "cause me to do Your will and the work You are going to bless." Then they follow where the Spirit leads them in accordance with John 3:8, *"The wind bloweth where it listeth, and thou hearest the sound thereof, but canst not tell whence it cometh, and whither it goeth: so is every one that is born of the Spirit."* The Spirit is in control. When man's intellect is in control, a believer thinks he already knows how to serve God. He petitions God to "bless what I am doing for Your church; it is the work You want done." Believers assume God's desire for them from intellectually perceived values found in Scripture, but God wants to direct every person individually by His Spirit. The attitudes of Spirit-led believers differ from the academic-led.

A reason why some intellectually based churches have abandoned Spirit-led faith—is fear. They fear dealing with a false spirit; in church, that could get embarrassing and emotionally messy. The Spirit of God is active, but His is not the only voice attempting to affect humans. That is why safeguards are written into Scripture. 1 Corinthians 12:3 and 1 John 4:1-3 are for testing the source of a spirit. A legitimate gift of "discerning of spirits" is also given to the church for further protection (1 Corinthians 12:10). Scripture never said to forsake spiritual leading; it teaches how to detect fraud. "Discerning of spirits" would be unnecessary if there was never a manifestation of a spirit. If fraud occurs, it must be exposed and dealt with. Though problems have risen in the past, the church is not to forsake its power source in order to incorporate something deemed better through human reasoning.

A cliché states, "don't throw the baby out with the bath water;" many churches have done that very thing. Much of today's church does not see the power of God illustrated by the early church. God didn't change. The change occurred within the church.

Behavior of immature believers was another reason Spirit-led focus was discarded. Though they manifested a spirit, they spoke and behaved carnally; they thought they were serving God but instead produced divisions in the body. There is a scriptural precedent for handling spiritual error; it is to **correct** the error (1 Corinthians chapter 14)—**not abandon biblical truth**. Instead of bringing correction to the error, some leaders began a more **educated** approach to the Scriptures. It was a path they initiated because Satan deceitfully led them onto it (not obeying God's Word illustrating correction). They didn't follow the biblical precedent of correction but instead deviated into their own solution. Because of the spiritual problems and fraud, "Spirit-led knowledge of God" soon turned into *theology*, "a study of God;" human reasoning was introduced into doctrine instead of **actively seeking** the Holy Spirit to illuminate Truth, part of His **scripturally described** activity.

Salvation soon developed into an emotional response to an altar call followed with recommended attendance at that church to be "fed." Certain churches advocated some degree of moral behavior, in others it was forsaken. The daily spiritual experience focusing on the life-leading Holy Spirit was replaced with intellectual understanding of God's Word. No longer would the Holy Spirit be portrayed as a voice in the conscience to guide believers. (Scriptures pertaining to the conscience are forthcoming in "The New Covenant" chapter.) By the conscience, the Holy Spirit could intercede to keep believers from error in word or deed;

183

He could also **encourage** them in approved speech and behavior.

By focusing on the academic approach to God, the **spiritual power** within the church also changed dramatically. Jesus said, *"Verily, verily, I say unto you, **he that believeth on me**, the **works** that I do **shall he do also**; and greater works than these shall he do; because I go unto my father"* (John 14:12). Aside from spiritual teaching, the works of Jesus were, exhibiting divine knowledge about individuals, giving prophecy for the future, exceeding the laws of physics—performing miracles, healing the sick, casting out devils and raising the dead. Those **forsaking** Spirit-led **gifting** and power **cannot do** the **above works**. That inability **forces** a question. "**Who** is in **error**—Jesus, or a church focusing on intellect rather than Spirit?" The answer to that question is obvious, *"...let **God** be **true**, but **every** man a **liar**..."* (Romans 3:4). Academic-led focus **opposes** what Jesus said and therefore was born of a spirit that combats against God; it seeks to deceive God's servants because **contradicting anything biblical** is motivated by the devil. When the Holy Spirit leads faith-filled believers, the encompassed Spirit-led churches will do the works Jesus performed; that is what Jesus said!

Many churches at present are too **sophisticated** to cast out a devil. Either they want to ignore the presence of devils, or they think devils have somehow vanished from earth between the time when Jesus cast them out, and the present. When did they stop demonizing humans? The idea they are no longer here does **not exist** in the Bible. The Bible declares they are **trying** to destroy every Christian. In 1 Peter 5:8, the devil continues to be the adversary, an **enemy** seeking to *devour* all Christians. James 3:7 says, *"...Resist the devil, and he will flee from you."* Churches have wandered into a fairytale land, believing they do not exist or need to be dealt with.

Biblically, the power of the devil is **only** restrained during

184

one time period, the one-thousand year reign of Christ (Revelation 20:1-3). After a thousand years, Satan is again loosed and allowed to intellectually deceive mankind one last time.

Instead of acknowledging the presence of demons, churches prefer assigning a medical term to everyone behaving like those biblically described as possessing them. Do today's leaders have the faith necessary to confront a devil? Aside from the church **not fulfilling** the functions Jesus affirmed, Satan **wins** a tremendous **victory against** the church. His legions of demons are **safe** and **free** to **remain** in whomever they are able to enter; **no one will cast them out**. Christians are now intellectual; they consider demonic exorcism to be nonsense.

Satan has been scheming to protect his demons for many years. Jesus taught His disciples that a demon established for a long time will **only** come out by prayer and **fasting** (Mark 9:29). Jesus had asked the father of the demonized son, *"...how **long** is it ago since this came unto him?"* The father responded, *"Of a child"* (v. 21). Then Jesus said *"**this kind**"* (v. 29, [existing many years]) will **only** come out by prayer and **fasting**. **Modern** translations **omit** the word *fasting* from verse 29. Previously, the disciples were casting out demons, but this one wouldn't obey them so they asked Jesus, *"...Why could not we cast him out"* (v. 28)? According to Jesus, the faith and lifestyle including the Christian discipline of **fasting** is necessary to cast out *"this kind"* of demon.

As Scriptures were re-copied, Satan was influencing mankind to disregard and omit pertinent words contained by original writings in an attempt to keep some of his demons safe. (Remember the *Alexandrian Text*.) That same gospel account is also recorded in Matthew 17:14-21; the NIV **omits all** of verse 21 requiring prayer and fasting (v. 21 KJV). That means the **only** biblical passages containing **existent knowledge** for casting out a long established demon were either **corrupted** to be **powerless**, or

completely removed from modern translation Bibles. **No one** reading only those Bibles **will ever** gain the necessary equipping knowledge it takes to victoriously confront a long established demon. These are not casual word omissions; they are precisely targeted attacks against God's Word in order to neuter the church's power and influence in the world; with no demonstrated power, the preaching of Christian faith is reduced into an intellectual debate to discern which religion of the world is the right one.

Much of the church is led by seminary trained pastors accepting modern translations to be superior to *Received Text* translations; the academics they learned will not lead them in how to deal with *"this kind"* of demon. If a "full gospel" believer's faith does not include the discipline characterized by a lifestyle of prayer and fasting, he will be powerless to help anyone demonized for more than a relatively short time.

Biblical omissions work along with the other devilish strategy to replace Spirit-led churches with academics-led churches. Those satanic victories sterilized much of the **spiritual power** in Christ's church. One result of these triumphs is that Satan's hordes can survive. Imagine the potential impact on the unsaved if all believers keep a clear conscience, are immersed in the Spirit and lead lives supplemented with prayer and fasting. They could zealously seek the Holy Spirit and His power to make every demon homeless. They would also be used of God to, *"...lay hands on the sick, and they shall recover"* (Mark 16:18). That passage was another target attacked by Satan. It is an additional *Alexandrian Text* omission. Believers need to know that God wants to use them for ministry to others. The **weakest** Christian is **supposed** to have more influential power than John the Baptist (Matthew 11:11).

How many people could be healed in this era if all the church applied what the Bible says? **Innumerable** souls could be won to Christ through the **display** of God's power.

186

Some may think study of Scripture is being discouraged because emphasis is presented for Spirit-led faith. That is not the case. In Spirit-led faith, the Holy Spirit is asked to lead and reveal the Truth contained in God's Word. He is asked to prevent all potential misconceptions of true doctrine. If there is not complete peace in the conscience, the Spirit is saying something is not rightly understood. Believers wanting God's Truth will dismiss reasoning of Scripture and wait until the peace of God shows them Truth. When the Holy Spirit reveals Truth, it is known deep inside the heart, a place where doctrines of men will never persuade anyone differently. They were taught by God Himself.

Since academic focus cannot exhibit any power of God, those following academics had to manufacture excuses explaining why Spirit-led focus is not for today. (The previously addressed viewpoints of why it ceased.) Evangelism through intellectually teaching the gospel became a major fruit of the academic focus. Evangelism is a wonderful work. If it were accomplished in power with spiritual signs following, its effectiveness would line up with Scripture. Jesus, His disciples, and Paul preached the gospel with **power following**. Paul said,

> *"And my speech and my preaching was **not** with enticing words of **man's** wisdom* [academics]*, but in **demonstration** of the **Spirit** and of **power**: That your **faith** should **not stand** in the **wisdom of men*** [academics]*, but in the **power of God***" (1 Corinthians 2:4, 5).

Many current leaders need to get serious about aligning with biblical example. They need to thoroughly repent of any willful sin, keep a clean conscience, begin a disciplined lifestyle of fervent prayer and fasting, continually petition God to be "endued with power from on high," and not neglect Bible study. They need to teach and advocate the Holy Spirit's power in church services and individual lives. God does not force His Spirit on anyone. He must be invited and sought for to be experienced. The pastor is the spiritual authority for a church; he is the one needing to encourage spiritual activity in his church.

If only the Holy Spirit could find churches longing to receive all He has for them. He would fall on believers as He did in the early church. Knowledge of spiritual gifting and power needs to be taught/preached and promoted to all believers. Leaders themselves may manifest several spiritual gifts, but the entire church is needed for all gifts to be represented. God will give several to each and **every** believer as He sees fit. The works Jesus did, the church will do; supernatural knowledge, wisdom, miracles, healings, casting out of devils and even raising of the dead will occur again. As believers walk in the **power** of God, the lost can be won through faith established by the *"power of God"* instead of only *"the wisdom of men."* (Note: after believers receive *"power from on high,"* they should be **careful of personal pride**. The end-time passage Daniel 11:34 indicates that *"flatteries"* given to those doing God's work can become a problem.)

Satan's tactics for warfare against the church are **no longer secret**; he plants deceptive thoughts in human minds; he corrupts Scripture; he academically neutralizes God's Spirit and Word as much as possible. He accomplishes warfare through twisting intellectual understanding of God's Word vs. Spirit-led Truth.

Individuals are able to grow spiritual fruits without the power gifting of God, but abilities to reach unbelievers and fight the devil's previous victories are **severely** diminished.

It seems the general attitude of believers is greatly affected without Spirit-led focus. Instead of knowing "how much closer can one walk with God," many believers want to know, "how carnally can one live and still make it into heaven?" Believers are almost dependent on hearing an uplifting sermon every Sunday, just to get through the week. Instead, they should be experiencing the fullness of the Spirit so that out of their bellies "...*flow rivers of living water*" (John 7:38, 39), enabling them to minister to others. The Holy Spirit's influence needs to be revived, promoted, and exhibited in the church again. The Holy Spirit and Bible are power sources for the church that have been victims of satanic attacks.

Maybe the church can learn from previous errors and not "throw the baby out with the bath water" again. There are good fruits in academically focused churches; they present biblical instruction in varying degrees, from fundamental to liberal. Some have a **reservoir** of knowledge just waiting for the Holy Spirit to effectively apply. Spiritual fruits producing character change can grow moderately. Love for others, evangelism, kindness, care for the needy, and faith in Christ can be major themes they incorporate. The church is **not** "all bad," as could be inferred from the above critique. A lot of **power** for influence to individuals and society has been neutralized. As presented earlier, error is to be corrected, rather than abandoning groups snared by error. Academic-led churches can repent and be revitalized by the power of the Holy Spirit.

The church needs Spiritual revival to bring it to maturity. Jesus is returning for a church without spot or wrinkle, holy and without blemish (Ephesians 5:27); only the Holy Spirit can grow believers into maturity. Those practicing academics need to be united and submitted to the active influence and power of the Holy Spirit. He will bring all required corrections to both individuals and churches.

> "*Finally, my brethren, be **strong** in the Lord, and in the power of his might*" (Ephesians 6:10).
> * * * * *

How does an individual believer comprehend when he is receiving direction from the Holy Spirit? **First**, His motivation **always** agrees with Scripture. He never gives anyone direction which is not scripturally approved. Second, He gives inner peace, not restlessness. Romans 14:17 reads, *"For the **kingdom of God is not meat and drink; but righteousness, and peace, and joy in the Holy Ghost.**"* The Holy Spirit produces God's peace within. When someone has inner prompting for biblical behavior accompanied by internal peace, the Holy Spirit is speaking.

Answers for requested guidance from God are normally given by two or three affirmations (2 Corinthians 13:1); most of the time those come from unexpected sources. Expect God to direct His people.

As believers interact with others, they may say or do something of which God does not approve. God will tell them of disapproval in the conscience, using unrest (lack of peace) to show them right from wrong. The same is true when they are confronted with spiritual teachings. No matter how convincing a sermon or teaching seems, if it doesn't "set right," do not readily accept it. Search the Scriptures in sincerity and prayer, under the guidance of the Holy Spirit. Colossians 3:15 tells us, *"And let the **peace** of God rule in your hearts....."* The Holy Spirit is peace, Truth, the witness of Jesus, righteousness, unity and joy on earth. He is waiting for every believer to understand more of Him so He can bring the full counsel and power of God to that soul.

His indwelling is so important and powerful that Jesus said, *"...he that is **least** in the **kingdom** of heaven is **greater** than he* [John the Baptist]" (Matthew 11:11). Jesus considered John to be the greatest of all prophets. *"Among them that are born of women **there hath not risen a greater** than John the Baptist..."* (Matthew 11:11). The lowest person with God's Spirit **in him** has more ability to serve God than the preaching and deeds of the best of prophets.

(Remember: believers will do the same "works" Jesus did.) The Holy Spirit living **inside** Christians is that important. The counsel and power of God can be manifested through any believer; age, gender, social standing, years in faith, level of spiritual maturity, etc., do not hinder God from moving by His Spirit. God and **His power** are in every believer!

Do not make the mistake of letting the pastor or church leaders function as your foremost "touch" with God. A relationship with God in that way is practicing old-covenant-style faith. The children of Israel wanted Moses to go near to God without them. Moses was their go-between man. However, God did not want a go-between; having Moses as their spokesman was what the **people** wanted. **They** wanted Moses to be their **only** touch with God. Exodus 20:19 says, *"... they said unto Moses, **Speak thou with us, and we will hear**: but let **not God speak** with us, lest we die."*

Christianity is faith in the same God of the old covenant; in the new covenant, God speaks directly by His Spirit and Word (the Bible). Listen for Him and have an honest relationship; that is His will. God is **not** looking for another mediator like Moses. Many people today still want a pastor or some other person to be their go-between. God has given His Spirit; He desires to know His people and for His people to know Him. Don't frustrate the urging of His Spirit.

Luke 11:13 says, *"If ye then, being evil, know how to give good gifts unto your children; how much more shall your heavenly Father **give the Holy Spirit** to them that **ask him**?"* **Jesus** said to *"ask Him."* If you are repentant and seek to know God, ask for the precious gift of **immersion** in the Holy Spirit. Now is the time. Your heavenly Father will grant your request.

If several weeks transpire with no apparent evidence of change, don't try to figure some reason of why the Holy Spirit is not the same as biblically described. Instead, ask the Father if something is preventing immersion in His Spirit. Ask repeatedly; if a wrong behavior continuously comes to mind, repent, confess it as sin and ask if anything else needs to be changed. Acts 5:32 says the Holy Spirit is given to those who **obey** God. Acts 2:38, 39 insure believers the gift of the Spirit is given for **everyone** and their children and even those *"...that are afar off...."* Keep asking; sooner or later you **will** receive immersion in God's Spirit. The disciples needed to wait at Jerusalem **until** they were endued with power; patient perseverance may be required. Continue with a repentant attitude toward sin and endeavor to keep a clean conscience. There are other existent spirits in the world that you do not want any part of. They will not affect someone sincerely seeking God.

If inner thoughts indicate others should pray for you, seek the laying on of hands from *Spirit filled* believers. Seek to experience what the Bible says; don't try to alter what it says to fit your experience.

Many people have an automatic transmission in their car. As a result, they may not notice the gear-shifting process taking place as they drive and speed changes. The same principle applies with a believer's **awareness** of the presence of the Holy Spirit. When someone comes to Christ (salvation), he is washed and the Holy Spirit **begins** dwelling within him. Since His coming occurs without their knowledge or immediate involvement, many believers **do not** acknowledge His voice when He tries to direct or correct them.

People driving a car with a manual transmission become very attentive to speed change and gear shifting because **they** are aware of and **involved in** the process. When Christians take part in God's procedure by repeatedly **asking** for the Holy Spirit, they **actively** take part and are therefore **more attentive** to His coming. By asking, they are expecting Him, listening and watching for Him.

The Kingdom of God

What is the kingdom of God? How important is it? Matthew 3:1-3 say,

*"In those days came John the Baptist, preaching in the wilderness of Judaea, and saying, "**Repent ye: for the kingdom of heaven is at hand**. For this is he that was spoken of by the prophet Esaias, saying, The voice of one crying in the wilderness, **Prepare** ye the way of the Lord, make **His** paths straight."*

Notice that John taught both **repentance** and the **kingdom of heaven**. By preaching those topics, he made preparation for the arrival of Jesus. Some Biblicists contend that John was an Old Testament prophet; therefore, teaching repentance (his baptism) is unnecessary for salvation. Mark 1:1 disagrees with that viewpoint: *"The **beginning** of the gospel of **Jesus Christ**, the Son of God."* Then the Scripture reveals John teaching **repentance** and the coming of Jesus (Mark 1:4, 7, 8). He said the "kingdom" is the **reason** people needed to repent. Preaching the "kingdom" is not Old Testament; rather, that theme is New Testament. John is the first New Testament prophet; he is not the last prophet of the Old Testament as he is sometimes viewed. Consider Luke 16:16, *"The law and the prophets were **until** John: since that time the **kingdom of God is preached**, and every man presseth into it."* The only reason *"...he that is least in the kingdom of heaven is greater than he* (John)," (Matthew 11:11) is that John did not live long enough to internally receive the Holy Spirit.

What did Jesus say when He began ministry?

*"Now after that John was put in prison, Jesus came into Galilee, **preaching** the **gospel** of the **kingdom of God**, and saying, The time is fulfilled, and the **kingdom** of God is at hand: **repent ye**, and **believe** the **gospel**"* (Mark 1:14, 15).

Additional Scripture continues to verify what was taught.

*"And Jesus went about all Galilee, teaching in their synagogues, and **preaching** the **gospel of the kingdom**, and healing all manner of sickness and all manner of disease among the people"* (Matthew 4:23).

Jesus sent His disciples to preach; what did He tell them to say and do?

*"Then he called his twelve disciples together, and gave them power and authority over all devils, and to cure diseases. And he sent them to **preach** the **kingdom of God**, and to **heal** the sick...⁶And they departed, and went through the towns, **preaching** the **gospel**, and **healing** everywhere"* (Luke 9:1, 2, 6)

The disciples were sent to **preach** the *gospel* ("the good news") of the "kingdom" of God. They confirmed teaching "**truth**" by casting out devils and healing diseases by the power of God. Do you think God intended for them to draw attention? That is certain; when legitimate miracles began, the people took notice. Their hearts were opened to hear a **message** confirmed through **miracles**.

What was so important about the gospel of the kingdom that it was confirmed by miracles? Is it the same gospel message much of traditional Christianity presently teaches? The majority of times, my experience from visiting many churches indicated it is **not**.

194

What is the *gospel*? Typically, the gospel is the message of the birth, crucifixion and resurrection of Jesus Christ, the atoning forgiveness for sin. It is salvation for every nationality—**everyone** who will believe. All of that is 100 percent true; however, **that alone** is not the **complete gospel** ("good news") from Scripture.

Paul refers to the gospel of **Christ** in letters of the New Testament. How does the "gospel of the kingdom" compare to the "gospel of Christ?" First, understand that there are not two different gospels. Unfortunately, many refer to the word *"gospel"* as an entity. *Gospel* is the translation of a Greek word meaning, "to announce good news." Everywhere one encounters the word *gospel,* it means—"to announce good news." There is "good news" in Christ! There is also "good news" in the kingdom of God!

Paul acknowledged the good news of the kingdom of God, but did not refer to it as the "kingdom." As a result, when churches began simplifying doctrine to basics, they overlooked the "gospel of the kingdom." The "good news" John the Baptist, Jesus, and His disciples taught was overlooked. The so-called "gospel" became overly simplified.

The message of the cross (Paul's good news), could **not** have been taught by Jesus' disciples early in ministry. Jesus' disciples **did not know** He would leave them via crucifixion. They were teaching the "gospel" without knowing about the atonement. What did they teach?

The "good news" of the kingdom is perceived using the Greek definition for *"kingdom."* The definition is "royalty" or "rule," which is derived from a word meaning "a sovereign, as a foundation of power." By substituting the definition for *kingdom* (royalty/rule), there is clarity for what Jesus, His disciples and John the Baptist taught.

Here is **"kingdom"** with its **definition** substituted for the following Scriptures: Jesus was speaking in Luke 4:43, *"And he* *said unto them, I must preach the* **[royalty/rule]** *of God to other cities also: for* ***therefore am I sent.****"* Jesus said **He** was **sent** to **preach** the **royalty/rule** of God. The Father **commissioned** Jesus to preach about this kingdom so it must be of enormous importance. Jesus gave instruction to His disciples in Luke 10:9, *"And heal the sick that are therein, and say unto them, "The* **[royalty/rule]** *of God is come nigh unto you."* **Miracles** occurred when teaching about God's royalty/rule to **confirm** its importance. Matthew 4:17, *"From that time Jesus began to* ***preach****, and to say, "****Repent****: for the* **[royalty/rule]** *of heaven is* ***at hand.****"* The phrase *"is at hand,"* means "to make near, approach." The royalty/rule of heaven is coming near, approaching. People are to **repent**, "think differently," because it is close. Luke 17:20, 21, explain why it is close.

> *"And when He was demanded of the Pharisees,* ***when*** *the* [royalty/rule] *of God* ***should come****, He answered them and said, "The* [royalty/rule] *of God cometh* ***not with observation****: neither shall they say, Lo here! or, Lo there! for, behold, the* **[royalty/rule]**, *of God is* ***within you.****"*

The unseen rule of God is **inside** humans. It is evident the rule Jesus spoke of is not simply a physical place where God is King, as some consider heaven to be. It **cannot** be preaching about the **cross**, because at that time His disciples **did not know** about the coming atonement. It cannot **only** be the millennial reign of Christ; He said it was ***at hand***, near. It is not **only** a place or thing. It is **also** a continuing action taking place **inside** believers—unseen to others. It is more complex than most Christians have ever pondered. His "rule" **has arrived**; it is **presently inside** His people. The millennial reign and New Jerusalem (heaven) are **future places** of God's rule.

This rule of God is in unity with the substance of the previous chapter. Remember **where** the Holy Spirit resides: He is **inside** Christians. For that reason Jesus said, *"Even the **Spirit of truth**; whom the world cannot receive, because it seeth him not, neither knoweth him: but ye know him; for he dwelleth with you, and **shall be in you**"* (John 14:17). Why is He inside Christians? The answer: To **rule**!

Notice the chronology occurring in the new covenant:

1. Jesus declared the **royalty/rule** of God was approaching; it would be **inside** believers.
2. Jesus stated the **Holy Spirit** would be **inside** believers.
3. Jesus atoned for sin on the cross.
4. The Holy Spirit came in power and changed disciples from **within**.

Before crucifixion, Jesus referenced the future by saying He **"shall** be in you." **Only after** the atonement would the Holy Spirit come and take residence **inside** of believers. Prior to the cross, no one—not even John the Baptist—could be washed clean enough for the Third Person of God to dwell inside and **cohabitate** a human vessel. The **Holy Spirit** is the **"rule of God,"** **dwelling within believers**; **He reigns**. The Holy Spirit is **"God in us."** The **ruling authority** for everyone born again has changed. Self must bow to the new authority. Believers have been purchased by the blood of Christ; a believer's life is not his own to live as he desires (1 Corinthians 6:19, 20). Self-will learns to **submit** to the rule of the Holy Spirit. While talking to Nicodemus, Jesus said, *"...Except a man be born of water and of the **Spirit**, he **cannot** enter into the kingdom* [rule] *of God"* (John 3:5).

A born-again Christian must purpose to think and act differently; he must be in unity with the unction of the Holy Spirit. Jesus said a believer's attitude must return to the trust and obedience portrayed by a young child.

> *"And Jesus called a little child unto him, and set him in the midst of them, And said, Verily I say unto you, **Except** ye be **converted** [literally, "turn quite around or reverse"], and become as little children, **ye shall not enter** into the **kingdom** [rule] of heaven"* (Matthew 18:2, 3).

Jesus purchased Christians; therefore, the rule of God **must** be established. A spiritual battle is taking place inside of **every** believer. Two natures desire to lead the activities of life. A believer has to fight to be obedient to his new ruling authority. He must **repent** of old thought processes and values of right or wrong. The **fight** is **spiritual** and begins in the mind.

That battle is described by Romans 12:2, *"And **be not** conformed to this world: but be ye **transformed** [literally: "metamorphose"] by the **renewing of your mind**, that ye may prove what is that good, and acceptable, and **perfect**, **will of God**."* The outcome of the battle determining how believers behave is won or lost by the **thoughts** they **choose** to ponder and obey!

For adults, yielding personal authority is difficult, but God has directed Christians to do so. Perception of the inner battle brings clarity to a verse of Scripture that is rarely recognized, *"And from the days of John the Baptist until now the **kingdom of heaven** suffereth violence, and the **violent take it by force**"* (Matthew 11:12). How can a Christian, a gentle promoter of **love**, **compassion** and **peace** become **violent**, and then **take** the "rule of heaven" by **force**?

After John the Baptist **proclaimed** the existence of the kingdom/rule, only believers willing to **fight** the **spiritual battle** of the **mind** could come under the **rule** of God. They had to be **violent**, **waging war within themselves** to have **leadership** of their lives

transferred to the **Spirit of God**. Their war is a **spiritual war** in the thoughts of the **mind**.

> *"For though we walk in the flesh, we do not **war** after the flesh: (For the **weapons** of our warfare are not carnal, but mighty **through God** to the **pulling down** of strong holds;) **Casting down** imaginations, and every high thing that exalteth itself against the knowledge of God, and **bringing into captivity** every thought **to the obedience** of Christ"* (2 Corinthians 10:3-5).

That is how Christians become **violent** and apprehend the **rule** of heaven by **force**. Read again the emphasized words in order: *war, weapons, through God, pulling down, casting down, bringing into captivity, to the obedience.* They fully explain what Jesus taught concerning the kingdom; from the time of John the Baptist, authority transfer can only be successful through violence (Matthew 11:12).

Early in ministry, Paul told the fledgling churches at Lystra, Iconium and Antioch about the conflict they will encounter to apprehend the **rule** of God, *"Confirming the souls of the disciples, and exhorting them to continue in the faith, and that **we must through much tribulation** enter into the **kingdom** [rule] **of God"** (Acts 14:22).

When Paul wrote concerning the function of the kingdom (rule), he **phrased** it **differently** than Jesus. He said believers were to be **led** by the Spirit—not the flesh. It was only a different way of expressing the **rule** of God.

> *"Because the **carnal mind** is enmity against God: for it is not subject to the law of God, neither indeed can be. So then they that are in the flesh cannot please God. But ye are not*

*in the flesh, but in the Spirit, **if so be that the Spirit of God dwell in you**. Now if any man **have not the Spirit of Christ, he is none of His**...[13] For if ye live after the flesh, ye shall die: but if ye **through the Spirit do mortify the deeds** of the body, ye shall live. **For as many as are led by the Spirit of God, they are the sons of God**"* (Romans 8:7-9, 13, 14).

Paul describes being "saved" as "being led by the Spirit" or "walking in the Spirit." It is the **same occurrence** Jesus taught in the **kingdom/rule of God**; they are the **same** but expressed using different terminologies.

In one of Paul's letters, he stated that he did not preach anything but Jesus Christ and Him crucified (1 Corinthians 2:2). Some churches have inflated that verse, building an entire doctrine around it **alone**—"Jesus and the Cross." By **focusing** only on specific Scriptures and **neglecting** others, God's full truth is overly simplified. Paul continued teaching after his statement about "Jesus and the cross;" he instructed believers about the presence and power of the Holy Ghost. Their faith should "stand" in the power of God (1 Corinthians 2:4, 5). Paul explained in great length in verses 10 through 14 concerning the Holy Spirit. His teaching about the cross of Jesus was followed by **instruction** about the **Holy Spirit**, the One ruling. That was Paul's way of teaching the **cross** and the **kingdom of God**. He instructed believers concerning walking in the Spirit, the power of the Spirit, spiritual truth, knowledge and discernment given by the Spirit, gifts of the Spirit and fruit of the Spirit.

In Romans 8:1 he said, *"There is therefore now no condemnation to them which are in Christ Jesus...* [the cross]." Immediately after that statement, he continued *"...who **walk not after the flesh, but after the Spirit*** [the kingdom of God]." Paul put the "cross" and "the kingdom of God" **together in the same verse.**

200

(Many believers only quote the first part of the verse due to another *Alexandrian Text* omission.)

No one gets one part of God without the rest of Him. God is Three-in-One. He cannot be divided by mankind; believers never have only a portion of Him. One cannot **only** receive the forgiveness of Christ's cross (salvation); they must also receive His Spirit (the rule of God). Believers must receive **all** of Him or they do not have **any** of Him. Paul reinforces the importance of the Spirit in verses 5 and 9 by stating that if someone does not have the **Spirit** of Christ, he does not have **Christ**. Without a doubt, Paul taught the kingdom/rule of God. That rule is applied by the Holy Spirit.

Paul revealed that he took active measures for the spiritual battle, *"And herein do I **exercise** myself, to have always a **conscience** void of offense toward God, and toward men"* (Acts 24:16). He *exercised*, literally, to "train" or "strive." (Jesus said the violent take the kingdom of heaven by force.) The **conscience** is the place the Holy Ghost gives a believer either **peace** or **conviction**. He speaks **directly** to them. The conscience is where Christians must "train" themselves and become violent to obey.

If believers miss the soft voice of the Holy Spirit during the day's commotions, He will speak again in bed after activities for the day are over. The conscience is heard the most clearly in the quiet, Psalm 4:4, *"Stand in awe, and sin not: commune with your own heart upon your bed, and be still. Selah."* God began His relationship with Samuel as he was going to bed (1 Samuel 3:9, 10). If God reveals an issue, promptly make it right.

How much has the rule/kingdom of God developed in you since first believing in Christ? A test can be used. Ask the indwelling Holy Spirit to show you; look honestly at the "fruits" produced. What are your character traits? Consider them to ascertain if "flesh" is your god, or if Jesus is your God. Please ponder Galatians 5:16-25, which say,

"This I say then, Walk in the Spirit, and ye shall not fulfil the lust of the flesh. For the flesh lusteth against the Spirit, and the Spirit against the flesh: and these are contrary the one to the other: so that ye cannot do the things that ye would. But if ye be led of the Spirit, ye are not under the law. Now the works of the flesh are manifest, which are these; Adultery, fornication, uncleanness, lasciviousness, Idolatry, witchcraft, hatred, variance, emulations, wrath, strife, seditions, heresies, envyings, murders, drunkenness, revellings, and such like: of the which I tell you before, as I have also told you in time past, that they which do such things shall not inherit the kingdom of God. But the fruit of the Spirit is love, joy, peace, longsuffering, gentleness, goodness, faith, Meekness, temperance: against such there is no law. And they that are Christ's have crucified the flesh with the affections and lusts. If we live in the Spirit, let us also walk in the Spirit."

One function of the Holy Spirit is to rule inside a believer. The position was **purchased by Jesus**. Believers actively and daily submit to the leading of the Holy Spirit in every behavioral action and word. They choose every day to be led by the living God of creation or by those things natural to man (social values and intellect). Christians' **actions reveal** their ruler. 1 Thessalonians 5:19 says, believers are capable of "quenching" (extinguishing) the Holy Spirit, so doing will cause them to live by the fleshly nature. Everyone desiring salvation has daily choices to make.

The governments of countries possess rule and authority over the people they govern. The citizens under those authorities must choose to obey the governing authorities. If some do not obey the authorities, the governments (nouns) still exist, but they are not "ruling" (verb) over those people. Unruly **people** are called **outlaws**. If Christians receive forgiveness for sin from Jesus, they must learn to submit to the rule of His Spirit so they are not outlaws against His government. Jesus told the parable of the "sower" to explain that concept (Matthew 13:18-23).

The general character of individuals changes if the Holy Spirit is in **authority** to **rule**. Believers do not behave the same way year after year. If believers understand the work of the Holy Spirit and cooperate with Him, they will be obedient to God by using **His** power...grace (an upcoming chapter).

The New Covenant

What do you understand the new covenant to be? Many years before Jesus, God foretold the new covenant through the prophet Jeremiah,

> *"Behold, the days come, saith the* LORD, *that I will make a* **new covenant** *with the house of Israel, and with the house of Judah: Not according to the covenant that I made with their fathers in the day that I took them by the hand to bring them out of the land of Egypt; which my covenant they brake, although I was a husband unto them, saith the* LORD: **But this shall be the covenant that I will make with the house of Israel; After those days, saith the** LORD, **I will put my law in their inward parts, and write it in their hearts; and will be their God, and they shall be my people.** ³⁴*And they shall teach no more every man his neighbour, and every man his brother, saying, Know the* LORD: **for they shall all know me**, *from the least of them unto the greatest of them, saith the* LORD: **for I will forgive their iniquity, and I will remember their sin no more"** (Jeremiah 31:31-34).

This covenant foretells of great forgiveness; God will put sin out of His memory forever—the cross of Christ. He said His "law" will **move** into the **inward parts** of His people. God's **law inside** believers is a portion of the **new covenant**. God's **law inside** people characterizes the conscience—the place God teaches His laws using peace or conviction. His laws are realized because of His indwelling Spirit.

The new covenant is found in Jeremiah 31:31-34 and Hebrews 8:10-12, 10:16, 17. His law is not simply the "written" law, but a "living" law.

Jeremiah 31:33, *"...I will put my law in their inward parts, and write it in their hearts; and will be their God, and they shall be my people."* God said once people are believers, He inwardly teaches them. Each believer will "know" Him—**all** believers including a child, scholar, laborer, teen, rich, the poor, etc. He is God **in** all of them. The "kingdom (rule) of God" (previous chapter) is **inside** believers, **fulfilling** this covenant; He *"...will be their God."*

The only way to experience complete peace inside the conscience is through the atonement of Jesus.

Hebrews 9:13, 14, *"For if the blood of bulls and of goats, and the ashes of a heifer sprinkling the unclean, sanctifieth to the purifying of the flesh: How much more shall the **blood of Christ**, who through the eternal Spirit offered himself without spot to God, **purge** your **conscience** from dead works to serve the living God?"*

People always felt guilty before Jesus came. With the blood of Christ, even the conscience is cleansed from fault; His blood takes away guilt. He will *"purge your conscience";* believers are free of guilt so they can be "led" of the Spirit to serve.

Hebrews 9:8-10, *"The Holy Ghost this signifying, that the way into the holiest of all was not yet made manifest, while as the first tabernacle was yet standing: Which was a figure for the time then present, in which were offered both gifts and sacrifices, that **could not make him** that did the service **perfect** [mature], as **pertaining to the conscience**; Which stood only in meats and drinks, and diverse washings, and carnal ordinances, imposed on them **until** the **time** of **reformation."***

205

The Greek definition of *reformation* is: "to straighten thoroughly or rectification." The Scripture is saying there is a time when **people** will be "**straightened**." When does it happen? The answer: When God's Spirit is **within** His people: *"And I will put **my spirit within you**...and ye shall **keep my judgments**, and **do** them"* (Ezekiel 36:27). That is the time of "reformation" (straightening). The time when people have a clean conscience and keep God's judgments is the same.

The **conscience** undergoes change and becomes significant when comparing the old and new covenants. In the new covenant Peter instructs Christians to have a "good conscience" (1 Peter 3:15, 16),

> *"But sanctify the Lord God in your hearts: and be ready always to give an answer to every man that asketh you a reason of the hope that is in you with meekness and fear: Having a **good conscience**...."*

Paul instructs Timothy the same way in 1Timothy 1:18, 19,

> *"This charge I commit unto thee, son Timothy, according to the prophecies that went before on thee, that thou **by them mightest war** a good warfare; Holding **faith**, and a **good conscience**...."*

Paul made his conscience a **prominent factor** for the defense of his faith. Acts 23:1 says, *"And Paul, earnestly beholding the council, said, Men and brethren, I have lived in all **good conscience** before God unto this day."*

Later Paul explains it is the "exercise" he applies to himself. He **deliberately** keeps his conscience pure, Acts 24:16, *"And herein do I **exercise** myself, to **have always a conscience void of** *offense toward God, and toward men."* That explanation is as practical as it can get; he is leading others by example.

He warns not to wound the conscience of a Christian brother:

1 Corinthians 8:9-12, *"But take heed lest by any means this liberty of yours become a stumbling block to them that are weak. For if any man see thee which hast knowledge sit at meat in the idol's temple, shall not the* **conscience** *of him which is weak be emboldened to eat those things which are offered to idols; And through thy knowledge the weak brother perish, for whom Christ died? But when ye sin so against the brethren, and wound their* **weak conscience***, ye sin against Christ."*

Some end-time leaders will abandon a clear conscience, teaching lies because of *seducing spirits*, and *"...having their conscience seared with a hot iron* [cauterized]*"* (1 Timothy 4:1, 2).

All people of faith are to keep a clean conscience. The Christian's conscience is thoroughly cleansed by Christ's blood. The conscience is where the new covenant is completed (God's law inside). It fulfills God's *"law in their inward parts."* Every believer is obligated to keep his conscience **undefiled** through obedience, even if the consequence is *"suffering wrongfully"* (1 Peter 2:19).

Please realize that nothing is **taken** away from **Christ** and the **cross**! Rather, the **fullness** of the **covenant** that His atonement purchased is in consideration. Some understandings for salvation are overly simplified, **omitting** or **not emphasizing portions** of God's covenant. Jesus' cross is not degraded; Jesus is **not jealous** of the Holy Spirit. Jesus wanted all believers to recognize all facets of the complete new covenant. He preached that it was near and then verified the teaching with miracles. He expressed further approval of the complete new covenant in John 16:5-7,

> *"But now I go my way to him that sent me; and none of you asketh me, Whither goest thou? But because I have said these things unto you, sorrow hath filled your heart. Nevertheless **I tell you the truth**; It is expedient for you that I go away; for **if I go not away, the Comforter will not come unto you**; but if I depart, **I** will **send him** unto you."*

The word *expedient* means "advantageous." Jesus acknowledged there is **more** than **His portion**; it is **good** and for a believer's **advantage**. Jesus died to atone for sin so that believers can be in God's presence through eternity. He also provided the **means** for the **presence** of God to **exist inside** Christians while they live, a **second segment** of the new covenant.

Churches emphasize Jeremiah 31:34, concluding, *"...for I will forgive their iniquity, and I will remember their sin no more,"* the atonement of Jesus. Christians must diligently hold faith in Christ; He is the only means for God's forgiveness of sin. The problem is that some churches observe the cross as the entire new covenant. It is a necessary portion of a larger divine work.

When Jesus said *"It is finished"* (John 19:30), **His** portion of the new covenant (the atonement) was finished. Consider what He said at the Last Supper to His disciples: *"For this is **my blood** of the **new testament** [covenant]; which is shed for many **for the remission of sins"** (Matthew 26:28). His **blood** was shed for the **atonement** portion of the covenant, the remission of sins.

He exposed the completion of the new covenant **after His resurrection,** *"And, behold, **I send** the **promise** of my Father upon you: but **tarry ye in the city of Jerusalem, until ye be endued with power from on high"** (Luke 24:49). Why would Jesus have His disciples stay in Jerusalem if the **covenant** was **completely**

208

finished on the cross? If the covenant was finished, there would not be **anything else** to come; it would be finished, concluded. He told them to stay because **more** was yet to come. Disciples being *"endued with power,"* would **fulfill** the balance of the new covenant **prophecy**.

The "finished-work" doctrine proclaiming the "cross of Christ only" for salvation, does **not agree** with other Scriptures. The **description** of the new covenant in Jeremiah and Hebrews, Paul's teaching about the Holy Spirit, and Jesus' instruction to His disciples all reveal an error in that extreme doctrine.

The conscience is involved in new covenant relationship with God. When listening for God during prayer, thoughts may turn to behaviors or attitudes producing guilt. Pondering excuses may **justify** the problems. If the same guilt topics come to mind repeatedly, God is undoubtedly showing disapproval of those behaviors or attitudes. Awareness of Scripture may also bring conviction to mind. Change those behaviors or attitudes confessing them as sin. That is *repentance*, literally: "to think differently." Make the issue "right" as soon as possible; a request for or granting of **forgiveness** may be necessary. If God approves of the changes made, that person will experience **peace** whenever those topics are contemplated. Past behavior no longer needs repeated **justification** for any issues. Ask God for His help (grace) to handle future trials.

The previous chapter addressed the kingdom of God—the rule of God taking place **inside** of believers. The chapter before that addressed the Holy Spirit, where He resides and what He does. The Holy Spirit (God **inside**), the "kingdom of God" (God's "rule" **inside**), and His new covenant (His laws written **inside**) are all parts one of another. United together, they comprise a unit functioning as **one**, even as the Father, the Son and the Holy Spirit are together in **One**. His Spirit is inside; His rule is inside; His "living laws" are inside via the conscience and His Word working in harmony!

209

Grace

Perhaps the most widely quoted application of the word *grace* is found in Ephesians 2:8, 9, which say,

> *"For by grace are ye saved through faith; and that not of yourselves: it is the gift of God: Not of works, lest any man should boast."*

That passage plainly says grace is a gift from God and is responsible for salvation. It works because of faith. So what exactly is *grace*?

I believe grace is one of the most misunderstood concepts in today's church. First, grace is given and cannot be earned. No one deserves God's favor. The definition of this Greek word yields more insight. By its Greek explanation, *grace* is "the divine influence upon the heart, and its reflection in the life." That definition may need to be repeated several times to grasp its meaning.

By definition, *grace* is one word that involves two distinct actions. For example, the English word "fetch" is similar in that way. If I tell my dog to fetch the stick I throw, I expect her to go after it and bring it back to me. *Fetch* is a word involving two distinct actions. The two actions of grace coincide; they are 1) the divine influence upon the heart, 2) which reflects in the life. Simply put, if there is no reflection or **result** of divine urging, it is **not grace**. If my dog failed to return the stick, she did **not fetch** it. Grace produces motivation for an outcome that **originates** from God and is then **performed** by believers. It is counsel from God affecting behavior. Where does divine influence move? It is **inside** Christians.

The Holy Spirit, the kingdom of God, the new covenant and

210

now grace, are **all** found **inside** of Christians. The word *grace* is utilized to describe **how** God's **divine work** is carried out. Grace defines how a human soul is changed from evil to good. It is bestowed because of Christ's sacrifice.

- God said He would make a **covenant** and His people would know Him and His laws in their inward parts (Jeremiah 31:33).
- Jesus declared the kingdom/rule would be arriving in His time (Mark 1:15).
- The **Holy Ghost** resides **inside** Christians (1 Corinthians 6:19).

Divine Godly **influence** is internal where the **thoughts** and **conscience** are affected. **Cooperating** with the divine influence is called *grace*.

The following chart shows by comparison, changes between the old and new covenant.

Old Covenant	New Covenant
The Holy Spirit comes "upon" and is with people.	The Holy Spirit is "inside" every believer.
The Law is carried out in the flesh (outside).	Grace is carried out "inside" believers.
The covenant is "outside" in the flesh—circumcision (by man)	The covenant is "inside" the heart—circumcision (by God)
God's rule was by prophets and priests from the tabernacle.	God's rule is inside the believer by His Spirit.

To better clarify grace, consider a condensed definition: "effective divine influence." Substitute it for the word *grace* in the following Scriptures.

Ephesians 2:8, *"For by* [effective divine influence] *are ye saved through faith; and that not of yourselves: it is the gift of God."*

211

Salvation is by effective divine influence.

Hebrews 4:16, *"Let us therefore come boldly unto the throne of* [effective divine influence] *that we may obtain mercy, and find* [effective divine influence] *to help in time of need."*

The throne of grace is the only place a person can **boldly** approach God. The Christian comes boldly when having trouble with obedience. He requests help, more divine influence when it is **needed**.

*"But we see Jesus, who was made a little lower than the angels for the suffering of death, crowned with glory and honor; that he by the **grace** of God should taste death for every man"* (Hebrews 2:9).

Jesus needed the *grace* of God to follow through with suffering. He laid down all of His power in order to become human. When He faced suffering on the cross, He asked the Father to *"...remove this cup from me..."* (Luke 22:42) and then yielded to the will of the Father. The Father sent an angel to strengthen Him. In verses 43 and 44, His sweat was like drops of blood. *"And being found in fashion as a man, he humbled himself, and **became obedient** unto death, even the death of the cross"* (Philippians 2:8). If Jesus needed *grace* for His flesh to obey God's will, Christians will require vastly more.

Jesus sits at the right hand of the Father to make intercession for believers. He is completely qualified to understand the frailty of human flesh and what is needed to overcome that weakness, *"For in that he himself hath suffered being tempted, he is able to succor them that are tempted"* (Hebrews 2:18). He understands temptation; He also knows how to be victorious and lead others in victory. God does not allow a believer to be tempted beyond what he can handle; God makes an escape from sin available,

> *"There hath no temptation taken you but such as is common to man: but God is faithful,* **who will not suffer you to be tempted above that ye are able***; but with the temptation* **also make a way to escape***, that ye may be able to bear it"* (1 Corinthians 10:13).

He promises to make an escape. Unfortunately, many do not seek escape or ask for help (grace).

Considering the meaning of *grace,* it is easier to understand how God works in the soul of man. The **indwelling power** of **God** induces true conversion from within; it operates to produce a holy vessel. That is why Paul was upset with the Galatians; they went back into justification by the "law." They *"...are fallen from grace"* (Galatians 5:4). They traded the "living law," the influence from the Spirit within them, for the written "law." The written law was only supposed to be a "schoolmaster" for bringing them into faith (Galatians 3:24). The law's function is to identify sin, making it *"exceeding sinful"* (Romans 7:13). That is why he called them *"foolish"* in Galatians 3:1. They forsook the Spirit to receive the written law that only identified sin. It was incapable of growing them to maturity (Galatians 3:2-4). Perfection (maturity) grows by *grace;* it is a gift from God.

Another "gift" is mentioned in Scripture: *"Then Peter said unto them, Repent, and be baptized every one of you in the name of Jesus Christ for the remission of sins, and ye shall receive the gift of the Holy Ghost"* (Acts 2:38). The gifts from God are internal: His grace empowered by His Spirit. They were purchased by Jesus; believers must think differently (repent) and overcome the natural behavior of fleshly mankind.

213

The instructions given in Zephaniah 2:3 and Luke 21:36 are for believers living in the end-time. Those passages reveal **WHAT** to do. Believers need to continually pursue those instructions with sincerity. With human nature, that is not possible. Humans become emotionally charged up if attempting behavioral changes. As soon as the "charge" subsides, so does commitment to change. For that reason, God's influence (grace) must be recognized. Believers that **recognize** counsel from God **cooperate** and produce the needed character changes. Because of God's inside power and presence, believers go beyond the ability of human determination. The Christian's heart will not be as "stone," but "flesh" (Ezekiel 36:26)—soft and pliable by comparison, ready to be sculpted by God.

The plan of God that prophets and righteous men of old have desired to understand (Matthew 13:17), is comprehended in the relationships between the new covenant, the kingdom (rule) of God, the indwelling of the Holy Spirit, and grace.

The new covenant declared what was coming; Jesus preached the *rule* of God arrived; the Holy Spirit began indwelling believers after the atonement; grace, *effective divine influence* brought fruits proving life changing rebirth.

Salvation exists in the *power* of God. He communicates with His people by His Word and Spirit. The conscience senses correction and reveals necessary change. Sensitivity for the presence, influence and power of the Holy Spirit cannot be emphasized enough; it is the substance of grace.

* * * * *

The previous chapters have shown **HOW** God works with believers. Revelation has shown **WHY** that is vital. Zephaniah 2:3 and Luke 21:36 revealed **WHAT** believers need to do.

UNITY

Understanding the huge jigsaw puzzle picturing the end-time is challenging. Human intellect fails more than it succeeds. The Holy Spirit is needed to continually bring light and perception for fitting pieces together. Someone may ask how. The use of some imagery is helpful to explain.

The scenes within this puzzle are formed by words (the Scripture); sometimes vague colors (metaphors) on puzzle pieces shroud clarity. Human reason can only form cloudy images. A *light bulb* for insight needs to be turned on. It casts light on fuzzy scenes, revealing they need to be rotated and placed in a different location. After a location change, it becomes evident that one of the pieces doesn't fit that scene. The same sequence continues for other scenes. Finally, when the colors are in place and each piece is in the appropriate scene, the scenes finalize a large completed picture.

The Holy Spirit is the *light bulb* producing light for spiritual eyes to see. The scenes from the puzzle require divine intervention for assembly.

There are other ways to assemble scenes. Applying the colors differently paints a diverse look; pieces won't connect smoothly and tabs need forced into place. The final picture does not look clear. The color and shape of the scenes are different and the picture is blurred.

The colors of pieces are words and the pieces assemble into scenes to fabricate events. The picture is the assembly of all scenes, producing a completed story. The omission of one puzzle piece distorts the completed picture.

All words in the Word of God need to be valued. Every topic has words pertaining to it, just like colors on puzzle pieces. If pertinent words are ignored, other pieces get bent out of shape and do not to fit well into the complete doctrine of Christian faith.

When a topic from God's Word doesn't have universal agreement, individuals have ignored words. That allows distortion in one direction or another. The distortion is the source for disagreement. **Ignored** words are the **root** of the problem.

Just like assembled puzzle pieces, the accumulation of all words shape the full grasp for scriptural topics. Again, one missing piece from a puzzle is quite obvious.

Individuals generally love to stay with the appearance of topics they have constructed. When trying to incorporate one topic with another, some won't fit together well; other pieces (words) have been ignored within those topics. Their completed doctrine is a jagged fit; various portions cannot blend together smoothly. To those individuals it doesn't matter; they can force unity into their doctrine through intellectual rationalizations, instead of complete applications of all pertinent words.

Disputing over doctrine has produced division in the Christian faith. The reason that problem needs to be solved is simple. In John 17:17-23, Jesus asked the Father for those who believe in Him to be one, even as He and the Father are One. When Jesus made that request, it became the Father's desire to answer it.

Compounding the divisive doctrinal problems, are the number of individuals aligning with contrasting groups. Like-minded seminary theologians teach pastors that doctrines conflicting with theirs are in error. If academic doctrines couldn't produce unity in the past, they won't in the future. Divisions continue to escalate instead of promoting growth toward unity.

Wisdom for apprehending the goal of unity is given in John 17:17, which says, *"**Sanctify** (literally: make holy) them through thy truth: thy word is truth."* The Word of God is Truth. Not one word of Truth can be ignored. If an individual forsakes part of God's Word, he is abandoning the resource that fulfills the request

216

of Jesus.

How can this seemingly impossible impasse be reconciled between believers? Jesus gave the answer: *"thy word is truth."* When every word of God is placed into a topic, *truth* will be the result. The appropriate color will be on the correct puzzle piece.

Accurate understanding for any questionable word needs to be researched. Then **all words** and related topics can be brought together to form a completed doctrine. The Holy Spirit illumines how all individual doctrines flow together to form a completed picture of the Christian faith. One scene from that completed picture is a church that functions as one body.

The problem continuing to hinder unity is that conflicting groups want their distorted topics to remain unchanged. They have been taught $2 + 2 = 5$ and want to keep it that way. Relation with other numbers shows there is error with that equation. Within distorted doctrines, relation with other applicable words from Scripture reveals the error.

Today, pieces of a body are trying to function as a whole. The eyes do not think they need ears; the hands do not think they need feet. 1 Corinthians 12:12-26 describes the body as being one, yet made up of many individual members. (Also see Romans 12:4-9.) The body needs all of its parts to function together as a single unit.

Again, the answer to the unity problem is *"thy word is truth."* If the divided body applies every word of God for every topic **without rationalizing**, a unified doctrine will result. Common instruction in the Truth of the Spirit grows a unified body.

The **focus** of importance on various topics within faith is not always the same; all believers are not the same part of the one body. For example: Baptists generally have a major focus on evangelism. Mennonites normally have a major focus on aiding those in need. Both of those are necessary within the body of Christ, and one should never degrade the other.

It is **basic** doctrine that must be **common** to all. The various works of service may differ. The eyes will understand the need for ears and hands for feet, **after fundamentals** are in place.

Though the focus may be different, unification begins as each group **resolves never** to rationalize **any** of God's Word. Everyone must let the Word of God say what it says and promote common basics. Then each group can appreciate others. The basics for doctrine are revealed by God's Word; humans do not need to figure them out.

> Hebrews 6:1, 2 state, *"Therefore leaving the **principles** of the **doctrine of Christ**, let us go on unto perfection; not laying again the **foundation** of repentance from dead works, and of faith toward God, Of the doctrine of **baptisms**, and of **laying on of hands**, and of **resurrection** of the dead, and of **eternal judgment**."*

Ponder those foundations: repentance, faith toward God, baptisms, laying on of hands, resurrection (eternal life), eternal judgment (hell). Those are **all foundations**, the common starting point for doctrine. The rest of faith's doctrine is built upon them. Hebrews reveals how disfigured doctrine has become. Many churches do not have those precepts as fundamentals for faith. They have embraced distorted topics somewhere along faith's pathway and must get back to basics. Numerous churches have totally abandoned some of the fundamentals. Those discards need to be addressed.

Presently, the love of God is emphasized by many churches. The love of God **is** to be taught, but **not exclusively**. Every sermon cannot dwell on blessings alone, and forsake all other biblical precepts. God also chastises His people (Hebrews 12:5-11); chastisement is for the good of the soul. It is a portion of God's love, but is not pleasant to experience. Numerous people want the more challenging parts of faith sugar-coated or neglected; pastors complying with that desire commit error.

God's full counsel necessitates elaborating on all statutes found in His Word. For instance, Psalm 111:10 says, *"The fear of the LORD is the beginning of wisdom. ... "* If one desires to become truly wise, **fear God**. In the New Testament, Jesus also taught about the fear of God,

> *"And I say unto you my friends, Be not afraid of them that kill the body, and after that have no more that they can do. But I will forewarn you of whom ye shall fear:* **Fear him, which after he hath killed hath power to cast into hell; yea, I say unto you, Fear him**" (Luke 12:4, 5).

Jesus spoke about **casting** a soul into *"hell";* that is the **same** as *"eternal judgment"* from Hebrews 6. Teaching on **hell** is appropriate and should **be taught to everyone early in faith**; it is supposed to be a foundation. More understanding can be built on the judgment of God (the reality of hell). Hell is something to be feared!

Some believe elaborating on only the love of God builds the church. Teaching about the fear of God didn't hinder growth in the early church. *"Then had the churches rest throughout all Judaea and Galilee and Samaria, and were edified; and walking in the* **fear** *of the Lord, and in the comfort of the Holy Ghost, were* **multiplied**" (Acts 9:31).

Churches that only focus on the love of God have very little power to influence believers to stop sinning. People continue sinning because of neglecting a foundation of the Christian faith.

At one time in the history of the church, the foundational precept of **repentance** was **not stressed**. The church fell so far

219

away from that foundation, church leaders sold *indulgences* (permits to sin) for money. Deserting this foundational truth happened during the Dark Ages of world history. That great error along with other doctrinal issues, initiated the Reformation of the sixteenth century. The Reformation gave birth to churches which are now referred to as Protestant; their founders **protested** errors in the doctrine of the established church (Catholic).

In this present era, foundational truth is again being rejected. Jesus' correction can be perceived through His letters to the seven churches of Revelation.

Many modern churches present a "light" salvation message; they teach people to accept Jesus as their Savior and ask Him to come into their heart. The problem is that they do **not** teach people to **repent** of **willful** sin. John the Baptist prepared the way for Jesus by teaching repentance. It was a starting point for faith in Christ, a foundation (as in Hebrews).

By relinquishing the foundation of repentance, churches have **again** wandered into error. Many churches emphasize giving money in order to carry out **ministry**, such as building funds, evangelism, social functions, charities, etc. As long as people support the institution by their giving and attendance, they have the churches' blessing. The churches are **not** taking a **strong stand** against sin; they declare that the people accepted Christ and are **saved**. That is exactly what happened before. The churches taught about Christ, took money and then turned their faces the other way so that people could sin (no repentance). That is the **same** fault initiating the Reformation, but currently in the disguise of salvation existing as a commodity one can keep, instead of a path that must be completed. Believers need to repent—not simply receive positive reinforcement while living in the same manner as before salvation. Repentance from **willful** sin **must** be taught! None of God's Word can be discarded.

"For if we sin [in a continuing sense] *willfully after that we have received the knowledge of the truth, there remaineth no more sacrifice for sins, But a certain fearful looking for of judgment and fiery indignation, which shall devour the adversaries"* (Hebrews 10:26, 27).

The foundation of *"baptisms"* (plural) from Hebrews 6, leads to another debated issue between churches. Ephesians 4:5 says, *"One Lord, one faith, one baptism,"* so there is apparent conflict between singular and plural baptisms within Scriptures. Leaders have chosen to adhere to one of the two viewpoints.

Baptism means to "make whelmed," i.e., the understanding of being fully or completely immersed. John the Baptist spoke in Matthew 3:11, *"I indeed baptize you with water unto repentance: but he that cometh after me is mightier than I, whose shoes I am not worthy to bear: he shall baptize you with the Holy Ghost, and with fire."* Utilizing other passages will reveal how baptism and baptisms can fit together in harmony.

The first-century application of that relationship is observed in Acts 18:25 and 19:2-6. At Ephesus, Apollos evangelized and baptized Christians with water for repentance. The people were saved, having only been water baptized. When Paul came to Ephesus, he inquired if they had received the Holy Ghost. They responded that they didn't know about that portion of Christian faith. Paul **baptized** them in Jesus' name. When he laid hands on them (another foundation), they received an outward display of the Holy Spirit. The same sequence occurred when Philip evangelized Samaria. Philip baptized new believers with water; later, Peter and John went to Samaria to lay hands on them so they could receive the Holy Spirit (Acts 8:12-17). That was the purpose of their journey. God displayed obvious approval of their actions; those new believers were immersed in the Holy Spirit.

Biblical examples establish great importance for salvation with *water immersion,* to be **united** with *immersion in the Spirit.* Observe what occurred: that is what the prominent apostles taught by their actions. It is also the reason Hebrews 6:1, 2 present plural baptisms.

When converts were saved and water baptized, the Holy Spirit took residence inside of them. When they learned about the Spirit, they were **immersed** in the Spirit through the laying on of hands. Baptism (singular) into the name of Jesus involves two baptisms: immersion in water and immersion in Spirit, after baptism of the Spirit is understood to exist. (Read Luke 11:13.)

For Spirit baptism, allow God to choose how He wants to make His presence known. Gifts of the Spirit can be another source of contention for believers. Ask God for Spirit baptism and let God handle the rest.

Faith in God, resurrection, and laying on of hands are other foundations that must be taught to all believers. Every biblical word concerning them is needed for complete comprehension. **After understanding** and **applying** the foundations of Hebrews 6, the child of God is supposed to **go on** to perfection (maturity).

The reference works of today were not obtainable in times past; most leaders only had an English **translation** of the Bible from which to learn. Not having the ability to research biblical languages led to miscomprehensions. For example, in Matthew 5:48, Jesus said, *"Be ye therefore perfect, even as your Father which is in heaven is perfect."* Logic says, "Jesus could not have meant what He said; only God can be perfect."

The English interpretation does not convey an accurate meaning for *perfect,* which literally means: "to become complete," i.e., "mature." Jesus was instructing believers to grow into **maturity** even as their Father is mature. Maturing **spiritually** (perfection) is not **impossible** for humans; however, the **English understanding** for *perfection* is **impossible**. Jesus meant **exactly** what He said, but many people have not understood what He meant.

An error in attitude has been the result of that misunderstanding. People who are of the Christian cliché mindset, "I'm not perfect—just forgiven," will never develop the **attitude necessary** for growth. They erroneously think there is no need to grow; they are "saved," and that is good enough. Their attitude fails because they **dismissed** a passage from God's Word and regarded it as unobtainable. Ignoring and dismissing portions of God's Word is the same root problem creating divisions within the "one body."

Jesus made a distinction between His followers; some He called *"lambs"* (spiritually immature) and others He called *"sheep"* (spiritually mature). He instructed Peter to *feed* (teach) **both**. That directive is found in John 21:15, 16. Paul also made a **distinction** within people of faith.

> *"And I, brethren, **could not speak unto you as unto spiritual**, but as unto carnal, even as unto **babes in Christ**. I have fed you with **milk, and not with meat**: for hitherto ye were not able to bear it, neither yet now are ye able. **For ye are yet carnal**: whereas there is among you envying, and strife, and divisions, are ye not carnal, and walk as men"* (1 Corinthians 3:1-3)?

The difference between the carnal and the spiritual is seen in their behavior. If believers are divided, *"walk as men"* and behave like the society around them, they are still *"babes in Christ"* and need to be fed milk (the foundations of faith). To be young in faith is to be a spiritual child; there is a proper time for the "milk of youth." To continue feeding only "milk" to one that is growing will become injurious.

*"For every one that useth milk is unskillful in the word of righteousness: for he is a babe. But strong **meat** belongeth to them that are of full age, even those who by reason of use have their senses exercised to discern both good and evil"* (Hebrews 5:13, 14).

If a child can learn and is given abundant knowledge, that knowledge does **not** produce an **adult**. It produces an **intelligent child**. The "**meat of growth**" must be added to the believer's diet, resulting in **spiritual maturity**. Other-wise, in behavior and character, people will remain in kindergarten while their knowledge of the Bible and length of time in faith indicate they should have graduated.

*"Who then is a faithful and wise servant, whom his lord hath made ruler over his household, to give them **meat** in **due season**? Blessed is that servant, whom his **lord** when he cometh shall **find so doing**"* (Matthew 24:45, 46).

That Scripture is found in Matthew's end-time passages; it challenges today's leaders to feed believers *meat,* not only *milk.*

Though sound biblical instruction is a necessity, academics are not solely capable of changing humans. Those who are led by the Spirit of God will develop the ways (spiritual fruit) of the Spirit.

*"For if ye live after the flesh, ye shall die: but if ye **through the Spirit** do mortify the deeds of the body, ye shall live. For as many as are led by the Spirit of God, they are the sons of God"* (Romans 8:13, 14).

Jesus talked about the development of fruit.

224

"And that which fell among thorns are they, which, when they have heard, go forth, and are choked with cares and riches and pleasures of this life, and bring **no fruit to perfection**. *But that on the good ground are they, which in an honest and good heart,* **having heard the word, keep it,** *and* **bring forth fruit** *with patience"* (Luke 8:14, 15).

Jesus obviously wants fruit to mature to perfection in the faithful.

Please note: spiritual fruit is **not** ministry or things that are done **for** God; those are "works" (Ephesians 2:10). Bearing spiritual fruit is **not** legalism. Leaders have repeatedly injured believers, even turning some away from faith by placing codes on dress, hair length, music, food and drink, etc. True, discipline is needed in all areas of life, but **humans** are not to draw the boundary lines. The Holy Spirit actively working in every believer's conscience, will direct whether or not something is acceptable to God. He counsels right behavior for wherever they live around the globe. He will lead and teach them; the Bible is His textbook.

Leaders need to instruct believers to **keep their consciences pure** and **listen** for **Him**. The Holy Spirit is to rule within believers—**not** the **verdicts** of **men**. Churches that fall into legalism, are trying to replace the *living law* of the Holy Spirit with their perceived values.

Fruit is the development of character. Through behavior Christians become the image of Christ. *"For whom he did foreknow, he also did* **predestinate to be conformed** *to the* **image of his Son**, *that he might be the firstborn among many* **brethren"** (Romans 8:29). The **will** of **God is** that His church becomes **Christ-like**.

There are those who are probably thinking of seminary or denominational doctrines that disagree with the necessity of

225

repentance and spiritual growth to maturity. They emphasize different viewpoints than those taught in this book. Ponder this: if at all times the **majority** of professionals and spiritual leaders are correct in interpretations they teach, Jesus would have been in error. The Pharisees, Sadducees, scribes and priests all opposed Him. Consider that again: if the majority of professionals and leaders have to be right, Jesus would have been in error. Do not blindly accept the teaching of educated men—no matter what their degree or title may be. Consider **all** of God's Word. Allow **God** to fully persuade you, *"Study to show thyself approved unto **God**, a workman that needeth not to be ashamed, **rightly dividing the word of truth"** (2 Timothy 2:15). Some doctrines you may believe are being challenged. Allow God to show you Truth and then teach it!

Scriptures such as Romans 3:10-18, Romans 7:14-25 and Romans 8:1 could be used to oppose the presented standpoint in regard to maturing. Consider additional passages of God's Word to help identify the Truth.

First, consider Romans 3:10, which says, *"...There is none righteous, no, not one."* Paul was paraphrasing passages from the Psalms and especially Isaiah 64:6, to expound on the natural, sinful way of mankind; he included those who follow the Jewish law. Doctrines teaching that Romans 3 indicates the impossibility for anyone to become righteous have misapplied the Scripture. Those verses are about sinners, Gentiles, the ungodly, and even those under the law. They do not refer to regenerate souls given rebirth through Christ.

After salvation, a person grows in righteousness. That righteousness is fruit which the Holy Spirit produces from within. No one can say fruit the Holy Spirit produces is *"filthy rags."* Any righteousness **before** rebirth was *filthy*. Behaviors, deeds and attitudes after rebirth are transformed by the Spirit; He doesn't produce *"filthy rags."* The description is **not** true of the work of

226

God within the maturing believer.

If a homeless, helpless person living on the street is picked up, cleaned up, given new clothes, a good job and hope for the future, he won't deny such deliverance. He won't declare that he is still filthy, homeless and helpless as in his prior condition. He would proclaim his new life and deliverance. He would have new hope and goals (rebirth).

To discover Truth, assemble **all** pertinent Scriptures so they function together like pieces of a completed jigsaw puzzle. Romans 3 will **only** fit in **unity** with **all** other Scriptures when it applies to the **pre-salvation** condition of the soul. After salvation, believers develop in righteousness,

> *"And he gave some, apostles; and some, prophets; and some, evangelists; and some, pastors and teachers; For the* **perfecting** *of the saints, for the work of the ministry, for the edifying of the body of Christ: Till* **we all** *come in the unity of the faith, and of the knowledge of the Son of God, unto a* **perfect man**, *unto the measure of the stature of the* **fullness of Christ"** (Ephesians 4:11-13).

Does this passage sound like human character traits full of *"filthy rags?"* No! Romans 3, is **not eliminating** the believer's active part in developing the fruits of righteousness. If that were the case, Ephesians 4:11-13 would never be fulfilled and the desire to mature in Christ would be destroyed. Christians must perceive the whole truth of God's Word in order to apply it.

Romans 7:14-25 is another passage that can be misunderstood. Some think believers can continue in willful sin and still be saved: *"For that which I do I allow not: for what I would, that do I not; but what I hate, that do I"* (v. 15). This passage of Scripture concludes by Paul saying, with his **mind** he serves *"...the*

227

law of God; but with the flesh the law of sin" (v. 25).

Paul would not deliberately sin, though the passage could be misinterpreted to imply he would. **Additional** Scriptures need to be considered to reveal what he meant. Paul said he brings his body *"into subjection"* (1 Corinthians 9:27). He could not sin **willfully** and still have his body under *"subjection."* It is **not** possible to do **both**. He said that he exercised to have a conscience *"void of offense"* toward God and men (Acts 24:16).

To resolve this apparent conflict, consider the context of Romans 7. He was not talking about committing avoidable, deliberate sin. He did not **premeditate** or scheme to be a thief, adulterer, drunk, cheater, a liar or perpetrate any other sin. He sinned in things done spontaneously—instantly occurring behavior without **time** to ponder responses. As a result, his **mind**, which served the *"law of God,"* did not have time to **control** the **impromptu** situation by **thinking** through his reactions. He reacted in his flesh, which served the *"law of sin."* **That is** the **conclusion** of the passage.

Look at verse 25: *"...So then with the **mind** I myself serve the **law of God**; but with the flesh the **law of sin**."* When he had time to think differently, he obeyed God. If he reacted from his flesh with no time to think, he served sin. That passage helps believers understand the difference between sin that is willful and sin that is not. It also explains how **repentance** from sin, to "think differently," really makes sense.

Everyone will experience the sin of their flesh, even though they do not sin deliberately. When viewed in that light, Romans 7 agrees with other Scriptures. That viewpoint also expresses what is meant in passages such as 1 John 2:1 *"...if any man sin...;"* sin is **not** to be commonplace in the Christian life.

A verse frequently used by promoters of a "light" gospel is Romans 8:1, which says, *"There is therefore now no condemnation to them which are in Christ Jesus....*" That **portion** of the verse is normally quoted. To quote and ponder only the first portion of this verse can be very misleading. Paul **qualifies** "*no condemnation*" in the second part of the verse: "*...who walk not after the flesh, but after the Spirit*" (Romans 8:1). For "*no condemnation*" to apply, Christians must follow the Spirit. What does it mean to walk after the Spirit? Paul answers later in the passage, "*For if ye live after the flesh, ye shall die: but if ye through the Spirit do **mortify the deeds of the body**, ye shall live*" (Romans 8:13). To "*live*," believers must allow God's Spirit to deal with their fleshly nature.

Those are some of the things Paul wrote which can be **misinterpreted** if one is not thorough in the study of Scripture. **Peter** said some of his writings can be **misunderstood**, to the **loss** of the **soul**,

> "*And account that the longsuffering of our Lord is salvation; even as our beloved **brother Paul** also according to the wisdom given unto him hath **written unto you**; As also in all his epistles, speaking in them of these things; **in which are some things hard to be understood**, which they that are unlearned and unstable wrest, as they do also the other Scriptures, **unto their own destruction**"* (2 Peter 3:15, 16).

There are no other Scriptures to which "wrong understanding" would more appropriately apply. Misapplying passages in Romans chapters 3, 7 and 8 could bring "*destruction*" to the soul. Peter continued, "*Ye therefore, beloved, **seeing ye know these things** before, **beware** lest ye also, being led away with the **error** of the wicked, fall from your own steadfastness*" (2 Peter 3:17). Peter was **warning** believers to **stay disciplined** in the faith. He basically cautioned Christians to avoid the *light* salvation message void of repentance. Passages in Romans can be misapplied.

Some churches base their understanding of salvation from the Book of Romans. They refer to their doctrine as the "Roman's Road for Salvation." According to Peter, they need to be cautious not to take any camouflaged detours to destruction that intersect on the Roman's Road.

> *"Wherefore seeing we also are compassed about with so great a cloud of witnesses, let us lay aside every weight, and the sin which doth so easily beset us, and let us run with patience the race that is set before us, Looking unto **Jesus the author and finisher of our faith**; who for the joy that was set before him endured the cross, despising the shame, and is set down at the right hand of the throne of God"* (Hebrews 12:1, 2).

Jesus is the **author** and **finisher** of faith. Jesus brings faith to completion (maturity/perfection). He does not bring maturity in the "great by and by," as some have been taught. The Bible is the believer's Instruction Book for behavior and faith while on earth. It is not meant to instruct people how to behave **after** these physical bodies die. If believers are not aware that maturity is a goal of Christ, they will not readily realize they need to cooperate with Him.

Jesus told a parable about a wedding banquet (Matthew 22:1-14), likening it to the kingdom of God. The guests originally invited would not come. The king made his servants bring in good and bad people from the highways. At the banquet, the king saw a man without a wedding garment, he made his servants bind him and cast him out of the wedding and into outer darkness. Revelation reveals the marriage of the Lamb to a bride who *"...made herself ready."* She was dressed in fine white linen which is the **righteousness** of saints (Revelation 19:7, 8). If people know about salvation, they must embrace behavioral changes so they wear a wedding garment, a robe of righteousness. Without it, they are banned from the wedding.

Whether for few or many, the leader is serving as a watchman for God's people. Review how God assesses the spiritual watchman in Ezekiel 33:1-9:

> *"Again the word of the LORD came unto me, saying, Son of man, speak to the children of thy people, and say unto them, When I bring the sword upon a land, if the people of the land take a man of their coasts, and set him for their watchman: If when he seeth the sword come upon the land, he blow the trumpet, and warn the people; Then whosoever heareth the sound of the trumpet, and taketh not warning; if the sword come, and take him away, his blood shall be upon his own head. He heard the sound of the trumpet, and took not warning; his blood shall be upon him. But he that taketh warning shall deliver his soul. But if the watchman see the sword come, and blow not the trumpet, and the people be not warned; if the sword come, and take any person from among them, he is taken away in his iniquity; but his blood will I require at the watchman's hand. So thou, O son of man, **I have set thee a watchman unto the house of Israel;** therefore **thou shalt hear the word at my mouth, and warn them from me.** When I say unto the wicked, O wicked man, thou shalt surely die; **if thou dost not speak** to **warn** the **wicked** from his way, that wicked man shall die in his iniquity; but his **blood** will I require at thine hand. Nevertheless, if thou warn the wicked of his way to turn from it; if he do not turn from his way, he shall die in his iniquity; but thou hast delivered thy soul."*

That passage contains a very solemn and powerful message. Paul considered that passage and received its warning:

*"Testifying both to the Jews, and to the Greeks, **repentance** toward God, and **faith** toward our Lord Jesus Christ. ²⁶Wherefore I take you to record this day, that **I am <u>pure</u> from the <u>blood</u> of all men**. ²⁷For I have **not** shunned to declare unto you **all the counsel** of God. ³¹Therefore watch, and remember, that by the space of **three** years **I ceased not to warn everyone** night and day with tears"* (Acts 20:21, 26, 27, 31).

Do the Lord's work with heartfelt diligence and in **complete** Truth! Apostles, prophets, evangelists, pastors, teachers, and elders are the watchman (leaders) of the church; they **will hear** the **whole** Truth of God, **if** they will **listen** for Him. According to Hebrews 13:17, leaders are held responsible for how they influence believers, *"...they watch for your **souls**, as they that **must give account**...."* (Also see James 3:1.) Judgment is coming and many people need to be warned to turn from wickedness.

If you lead others, please contemplate the ones **entrusted** to your care—even if it is only your family. Are they growing in the fruits of godliness to become Christ-like? In Mark 4:20, Jesus said believers will grow fruit—thirty fold, some sixty and some one hundred. Think about that: after salvation, people exceed any natural goodness they may possess by a minimum of thirty times and as much as one hundred times. There are a lot of good changes taking place in their character.

Jesus said things that many leaders avoid, acting as though the verses do not exist:

"I am the true vine, and my Father is the husbandman.

232

*Every branch **in me** that **beareth not fruit he taketh away:** and every branch that **beareth fruit,** he **purgeth** it, that it may **bring forth more fruit**"* (John 15:1, 2).

Purgeth means to "cleanse" or "prune." When a vine is pruned, any unproductive lead on the main vine is cut away. That is what happens when God chastises one of His servants. He works to remove behavior or attitudes that are unproductive in godliness. Jesus' words are Truth. Teach others in such a way that His Words bear good fruit in the ones hearing you.

Do not allow **any part of God's Word** to be **nullified** by the theologies of men! The Pharisees and Sadducees reasoned away and nullified commandments of God (Matthew 15:3-6); Christians must be careful to learn from their mistake so they do not repeat the error.

Ephesians 4:11-13, as well as the following seven Scriptures indicate that believers are to mature, putting aside the sin nature to become Christ-like. As you read them, look for **proper application** and **agreement** between them:

"Having therefore these promises, dearly beloved, let us cleanse ourselves from all filthiness of the flesh and spirit, perfecting holiness in the fear of God" (2 Corinthians 7:1).

"Be ye therefore perfect, even as your Father which is in heaven is perfect" (Matthew 5:48).

"Follow peace with all men, and holiness, without which no man shall see the Lord" (Hebrews 12:14).

"I beseech you therefore, brethren, by the mercies of God, that ye present your bodies a living sacrifice, holy, acceptable unto God, which is your reasonable service. And be not conformed to this world: but be ye transformed by the

renewing of your mind, that ye may prove what is that good, and acceptable, and perfect, will of God" (Romans 12:1, 2).

"Nevertheless the foundation of God standeth sure, having this seal, The Lord knoweth them that are his. And, let every one that nameth the name of Christ depart from iniquity" (2 Timothy 2:19).

"As obedient children, not fashioning yourselves according to the former lusts in your ignorance: But as he which hath called you is holy, so be ye holy in all manner of conversation" (1 Peter 1:14, 15).

"Whom we preach, warning every man, and teaching every man in all wisdom; that we may present every man prefect in Christ Jesus" (Colossians 1:28).

Abundant use of Scripture was intentional to emphasize that "growth in **righteousness**" is doctrinal Truth. The above-listed Scriptures are not exhaustive, more could be included. Maturity comes when a believer chooses to cooperate with the Spirit of God. The people who come to Jesus need to know that Jesus is not simply the **Author**, but He is also the **Finisher** of faith.

If a leader **ignores** vital facts while teaching, he **misrepresents** the truth. What he says may be **portions** of truth, but **disregarded** facts **distort** complete understanding. Truth that is partial is deception and deception is a lie, i.e., the fables of the end-time in 2 Timothy 4:4. Please do not handle the Word of God deceitfully. Teach **all** of God's Word—not just light concepts people prefer. Some people may get offended. If you are a pastor, you might have to downsize a building. People can head for the door when you preach about living righteously and against sin. Make the choice: do you want to serve the **religion** of men or **Truth** of God? If you will serve God, He will be the source for your **needs**, **not** necessarily **wants**.

234

Obviously, not everyone reading this is currently in leadership. The rest of believers need to keep leadership accountable to the full Truth of the Word of God. Hopefully, most leaders are humble enough to cooperate with God in establishing full Truth in churches.

If there is no church within commuting distance teaching and promoting full biblical truth, ask God if He would have you start a home fellowship with other sincere lay believers. Globally, a huge number of Christians still meet in their homes.

*"**Preach the word**; be instant in season, out of season; **reprove, rebuke, exhort with all longsuffering and doctrine**. For the time will come when they will **not endure sound doctrine**; but after their own lusts **shall they heap to themselves teachers**, having itching ears; and they shall **turn away their ears from the truth**, and shall be turned unto fables"* (2 Timothy 4:2-4).

*"Therefore seeing we have this ministry, as we have received mercy, we faint not; But have renounced the hidden things of dishonesty, not walking in craftiness, **nor handling the word of God deceitfully**; but by manifestation of the truth commending ourselves to every man's conscience in the sight of God"* (2 Corinthians 4:1, 2).

* * * * *

Unity in Christian faith is not accomplished exclusively by researching the Bible. Unity through the Holy Spirit is necessary; He moves in the meek by love (Ephesians 4:2, 3). Leaders must resist the urge to follow the academic path of their past when error is revealed to them. Humble leaders will allow the Word and the Holy

Spirit to mold doctrine into a completed picture. Each leader will then possess a distortion-free puzzle, all of which will look the same.

Never start down the trail called "compromise of God's Word;" it only leads to further compromise. Humans currently add reasoning to Scripture, thereby altering meaning. That practice leads into inaccuracy. If one doesn't understand a portion of the Scripture, he simply doesn't understand it yet. That is not a flaw. A problem arises when he tries to instruct others by a humanly reasoned precept.

> *"Every word of God is **pure**: he is a shield unto them that put their trust in him. **Add thou not unto his words**, lest he reprove thee, and **thou be found a liar"** (Proverbs 30:5, 6).

When believers are led in the full counsel of Truth, the unity of the one body will follow. Multiple believers functioning as one body is not impossible. All parts of the body will join together to form the bride of Christ. It all starts with **uncompromised** application of God's Word being lived through His Spirit.

Spirit-directed living is required for successful living as "one." The Spirit-led Word of God trains humans in truth, and then the Spirit influences behavior. His moving inside believers is called *grace*—"effective divine influence." The grace of God is realized in the *conscience*, which is where the Spirit speaks directly to every Christian.

A huge amount of the Christian faith depends on the Holy Spirit. He produces inside unction to avoid sin; He promotes the work of God, the deeds believers perform for the church (Titus 3:8). He teaches and gives gifts for administration, exhibition of power, and service for others that is beyond normal initiative and ability. By His influence, believers serve with an attitude of love for others—not a cliché but biblical love described in 1 Corinthians 13. The Spirit brings unity into the "body" because **He is common** to every believer. He causes the body, consisting of many members, to function as "one body" because He is directing the lives of all believers. When mature Christians obey Him, the church will be "one."

> *"Now I beseech you, brethren, by the name of our Lord Jesus Christ, that ye **all speak the same thing**, and that there be **no divisions among you**; but that ye be **perfectly joined** together in the **same mind** and in the **same judgment**"* (1 Corinthians 1:10).

Today's churches are immature, carnal churches. They exist with varying identities and doctrines, so they are carnal.

> *"For **ye are yet carnal**: for whereas there is among you envying, and strife, and **divisions**, are ye not carnal, and walk as men? For while one sayeth, I am of Paul; and another, I am of Apollos; are ye not carnal"* (1 Corinthians 3:3, 4)?

When Christians grow into maturity, becoming spiritual Christians, divisions of carnality end; **overcomers** will emerge from the seven different churches of Revelation. The "body of Christ" will function as a unit. Jesus' prayer to the Father for His people to be unified will be answered.

What would the Godhead be like if They followed the lack of unity displayed by today's Christian church? The church needs to change. Please be part of the solution, rather than the problem. Teach the full counsel of God being lived through the Spirit and guided by the conscience.

The unity of one body and mind is a common New Testament doctrine found in the following passages: John 17:20-23; Romans 12:4-10; 1 Corinthians 1:10, 12:12-27; 2 Corinthians 13:11; Galatians 3:26-29; Ephesians 2:14-16, 4:2-4; Philippians 1:27, 2:2; Colossians 2:19, 3:15; 1 Peter 3:8, 4:1. Unity is a goal for the mature body of Christ.

Some well-meaning believers understand the need for unity and focus on some basic, general doctrines to establish harmony between churches. They evade portions of God's Word that produced division in the past. Baptism in the Holy Spirit is an example. Thereby a problem is presented; unity is promoted in the church, but at the cost of the **complete** counsel from the One **owning** the church. The ones attempting unification say it is justified because they are loving the brotherhood. Jesus said a believer must love **Him** even above members of his own family (Matthew 10:37).

According to John 1:1, Jesus is the Word of God; the writing of the spoken and inspired Word of God became the Bible; the completed Bible represents Christ. What part of Christ should believers ignore so that they can get along with one another? The answer: **no part of Christ is to be ignored**. All believers are to line up with all parts of Christ. Believers must love Jesus first and the brotherhood of faith, second. Believers must embrace all of the Word, allowing complete Spirit-led understanding to reconcile conflicts. Only submissive, humble servants will permit the Holy Spirit to make the necessary changes in doctrines so that He establishes unity among brethren. That is the unity Jesus requested from the Father.

God will instruct all leaders humble enough to hear and receive the Truth from Him (Ezekiel 33:7). When humble leaders gather together, doctrines will be the same. The Holy Spirit only teaches Truth—not multiple interpretations for Scriptures.

In the mature church, leaders encourage believers to receive instruction from other Christian leaders or use their abilities to serve others; they won't have to be of the same denomination. Under guidance of the Holy Spirit, believers are guided where to go to receive a teaching they may need or to use gifts that they possess. Pastors will understand the church belongs to Jesus and He leads every individual, edifying the whole body; they will not fear losing "their" church members to another congregation. The body is to function as "one;" each member cares for the others. Jesus is responsible to care for His church; leaders must listen to Him.

* * * * *

This writing is presented, knowing all leaders will give an account to God for the things they preach or teach.

Only the Holy Spirit can bring assurance that correct doctrine is presented here. *"Howbeit when he, the Spirit of truth, is come, **he will guide you into all truth**... "* (John 16:13). Never replace the peace and unction of the Holy Spirit with any teaching by men. When teachings differ, study to find the truth and depend on the Holy Spirit; He will teach you. His teaching will surpass all intellectual understanding. **His** Truth is deep inside. *"But the Comforter which is the Holy Ghost, whom the Father will send in my name, **he shall teach you all things**, and bring all things to your remembrance, whatsoever I have said unto you"* (John 14:26). The Holy Spirit will always agree with right interpretation for all the inspired words of the Bible. **What is He saying to you**? Are viewpoints communicated through this book "truth," or are other opinions expressing the Christian faith true? Ask God for the Truth!

Appendix
GROWTH

The following list is an attempt to briefly phrase accurate doctrine for **growing** in the faith of Christ:

- Repent of all voluntary, willful sin.
- Ask Jesus for forgiveness and confess every sin perceived.
- Make Jesus both Savior and Master, deserving worship and obedience.
- Get water baptized. (Immersion is the biblical standard.)
- Ask God to immerse you in the Holy Spirit.
- Ask for the Holy Spirit to direct your life, pray and follow His direction in accordance with **all** of His Word, which you need to read regularly.
- Obey His voice when He speaks in your conscience to develop Godly character.
- Day by day, week by week, and year by year **do** the works of service for Him as He directs you.

God revealed His purposes for a believer's development through prophecy. Consider His intent as expressed in Ezekiel 36:26, 27:

> *"A new heart also will I give you, and a new spirit will I put within you: and I will **take away the stony heart** out of your flesh, and I will give you an **heart of flesh**. And I will put **my spirit within you**, and **cause** you to **walk in my statutes**, and ye shall keep my judgments, and do them."*

Peter said that **prophecy** is a "sure word," establishing Truth even more than a miraculous voice speaking from heaven (2 Peter 1:17-19). Solemnly ponder the above prophecy!

Probable Sequences of Events

First seal: Wrong doctrine taught by leaders (Matt. 24:5; 2 Tim. 4:3,4; Rev. 6:2) Opened

Second seal: Wars, famines, pestilences, earthquakes (Matt. 24:6, 7; Rev. 6:4)   Presently opening

Correction to churches: (Rev. chapters 2-3)   Current

Saints of God sealed, provided for: (Rev. 6:6, 7:3; Luke 17:36, 37; Isaiah 65:13, 14) Will occur before earth is "hurt" to produce famine during the third seal.

Third seal: Great famine (Matt. 24:7; Rev. 6:5, 6)

2 witnesses of God begin: (Rev. 11:3, 14:9, 10)

Fall of Babylon: Crash of world economy (Rev. 17:3, 16, 17; 18:21)   Leads to governmental change

Fourth seal: Many killed (Rev. 6:8)

Rise of first beast (Rev. 13:1, 5; 17:10)

God is publically blasphemed (Rev. 13:6; Dan. 11:36)

2 witnesses killed (Rev 11:7)

Fifth seal: Martyrdoms of saints (Rev. 6:11, 11:7, 13:7, 10; Matt. 24:9)

Rise of second beast (Rev. 13:11-12, 17:11; 2 Thess. 2:9-12)

Captive martyrs witnessing; killed for refusing the mark (Luke 21:13, 15, 19; Rev. 13:15, 20:4)

Seventh seal (sixth to follow): Seven trumpet and vial wrath judgments upon ungodly (Rev. 8:6, 16:1)

Beginning of **seventh** trumpet and vial judgment: Jesus' return, saints raptured, resurrection of dead (1 Thess.4:15-17; Rev.10:7, 16:15)

Sixth seal opened and unifies with seventh judgment (above): Jesus' return (Rev. 6:12-17, 19:11-16)

1,000-year reign of Jesus (Rev. 20:6; Isaiah 11:1-9)

Great White Throne Judgment (Rev. 20:11, 12; Daniel 12:1, 2)

New Jerusalem, new heaven and new earth (Rev. 21:1-2; Isaiah 65:17-25)

Eternity with God (Rev. 22:1-5)

Addendum

Though this subject matter does not pertain to this book, valuable information is contained within Revelation regarding people misusing drugs. Sometimes the ones using them justify their habit by stating, "God does not disapprove; after all, it is not written in the Bible." Conversely, Revelation 9:21 reads: *"Neither repented they of their murders, nor their **sorceries**, nor of their fornication, nor of their thefts."* The context of this verse addresses behaviors God **disapproves** of. The words used were written in the dialect of the era of translation, rather than modern-day vernacular.

The word translated *sorceries* is the Greek word *pharmakeia* (Strong's #5331), meaning "**medication.**" The English word *pharmacy* is derived from this Greek word. In the 1380s when John Wycliffe first translated the Bible into English, a person desiring "recreational medication" had to get it from a sorcerer or witch. In that era *pharmakeia* was translated as "sorcery" or "witchcraft"—the use of medication within a negative context. In today's language, that application is referred to as "drugs." God does not approve of drug use. He equates it with murder, fornication and theft. The same Greek word is translated "witchcraft" in Galatians 5:20. According to verse 21, people continuing this behavior will **not** be included in God's kingdom (no salvation). One would think **all** modern translations would be accurate with this very important and currently relevant topic, but they are not. In searching a dozen modern translations, the *Common English Bible* correctly conveyed *pharmakeia* as drug use in Revelation 9:21. *God's Word* translation is accurate in Galatians 5:20. **Only** the above translations for those two verses reveal the truth about drugs.

If you know someone struggling with drug abuse, please use this information to help convince them to stop using drugs.

Additional copies of this book can be purchased at
http://www.amazon.com/dp978-1986245272

Author can be contacted at openrevelation@hotmail.com

243

Made in the USA
Monee, IL
15 March 2020